LIVE AMONG THEM

LIVE AMONG THEM

Building Relationships for Jesus

MARK S. DISBROW

Mark S Disbrow

CONTENTS

Copyright © 2022 by Mark S. Disbrow
ISBN: 9780578296586   epub: 9780578296593

First Printing, 2022

Mark S. Disbrow
77 Navajo Cir.
Pagosa Springs, CO 81147
mark@amazinggraceco.org

Acknowledgments

I wish to acknowledge Nancy Rea who helped me formulate some of these real-world practices that are written in this book. An immense amount of gratitude goes to Helene Smith who edited the book for me.

Thank you also to my wife of 30 years, Adrienne, a reluctant pastor's wife, for her support in 20 years of ministry. It is written in honor of Jesus Christ, my Lord and Savior, who picked me up from the mire and set me on the path to life.

"As each one has received a special gift, employ it in serving one another as good stewards of the manifold grace of God" 1 Peter 4:10

"How lovely on the mountains Are the feet of him who brings good news, Who announces peace And brings good news of happiness, Who announces salvation, And says to Zion, "Your God reigns!" Isaiah 52:7

Preface

I wrote this after nearly 20 years of ministry.

Live Among Them is a timeless principle I picked up somewhere along the line and followed intuitively. This lifestyle excited me. My ministry experiences brought pure adventure, intense adventure.

Prior to being called by God into ministry, I had been a stay-at-home homeschooling dad to our two small children. I fixed computers and created free websites for churches as a ministry. Before that season I worked as a real estate and finance businessman.

My first endeavor in ministry resulted in an outdoor church plant geared towards reaching the unsaved and unchurched, the vacationers from Los Angeles, and rock climbers from around the world. My wife, Adrienne, and I held church outdoors in campgrounds, rock climbing venues, and even in cow pastures.

In 2011, we moved to a small mountain town and bought a house on 10 acres in a subdivision known by locals as the lawless West.

I wrote this book to challenge and encourage all—pastors,

missionaries, lay people—who minister to the lost, poor in spirit, and lawless.

This book is intended to be less about me and more about Jesus—not an autobiography. You'll find a blend of teaching the method of "Living Among Them" and stories of real-life ministry. The names, identities, and minor details have been changed so as not to reveal things people may not want publicly known.

Feel free to read chapters out of order based on your topical interest. I hope that I can be a catalyst for your church to figure out how to do ministry like Jesus. The old way. And if you are already serving in this manner, I pray this book encourages you to keep on. Don't let the setbacks or seeming lunacy stop you!

"Therefore, since we have so great a cloud of witnesses surrounding us, let us also lay aside every encumbrance and the sin which so easily entangles us, and let us run with endurance the race that is set before us, fixing our eyes on Jesus, the author and perfecter of faith, who for the joy set before Him endured the cross, despising the shame, and has sat down at the right hand of the throne of God. Hebrews 12:1-2

CHAPTER 1

First, The Setting

- The Modern Church
- The Setting
- Stories of Samaria
- The Call

THE MODERN CHURCH

When you think of church, what comes to mind—a beautiful building, wonderfully adorned with stained glass and wooden pews, facing a stage with an ornate altar? Regardless of the structure, we think of church as a place we go each Sunday morning for an hour. People are dressed in their finest clothing and on their most polite and proper behavior. There is an element of uniformity in them. The pastor is dressed in a suit or other religious garb and set apart up front seated on a regal chair. Frequently, he is in a hidden room somewhere and everyone quietly waits for him to enter as the musicians prepare to play.

This book will most assuredly mutilate that fine vision.

Live Among Them is about literally choosing to live among the most unruly, unchurched, foul-mouthed, needy, spiritually poor people you could gather. Sprinkled into this lump are true gems of people who wholeheartedly love Jesus. Blessed are the poor in spirit.

THE SETTING

The setting is a subdivision that I will call Samaria. The neighborhood is comprised of one to four acre parcels with custom "homes". The church building is a pole barn finished inside with rough wood, laminate wood floor, large metal wood-stove, and seating arranged generally in a circle. Depending on when you enter. Often seats are "not-arranged". Folding tables are set up with chairs around them. There is a loft with a wrought iron spiral staircase. The bathrooms are in an outdoor shed a couple feet from the barn. This church is situated on 10 acres, which includes a log cabin house where the author and family live. The property is graced with an abundance of evergreen trees. The subdivision roads and the parking area are gravel.

STORIES OF SAMARIA

Early on in this ministry, a church member repaired the water system on the property. We talked as he climbed into this truck to leave. He backed out as another truck came up the driveway with a man and woman inside. The man wearing a trench coat popped out and proceeded to walk up to me. He threw his arms around me in a bear hug. He lifted me up about a foot off the ground and began to yell, "I love you." He was emotional and loudly talking. Meanwhile, the contractor hesitated as he backed down the driveway not sure if he should stay to help me or go home. My wife heard the commotion from inside the house wondering if she should call 911. I felt embarrassed, caught up in this bear hug with a drunk telling me he loves me. So naturally, I wrapped my arms around him and told him "I love you too." He let me down and asked if he could play the guitar for me because he wanted to play in church. I politely suggested now wasn't the time. He pulled out his guitar case and began to run animatedly around his truck, his coat tails flying in all manner of agitation. I was witnessing a demon-possessed man.

On a beautiful fall day I walked up my driveway from the church to my house. I heard a whizzing noise in the branches about two feet above me. I looked up and around attempting to figure out the source of the noise. I heard more whizzing and put two and two together. Bullets! My neighbor, who at this time hated me and our church, was shooting his gun. After the sheriff showed up to take the report and quiz my neighbor, I walked the 200 yards from the house over to the backside of the church to check on the homeless guy staying there. I told him of my near-death experience and he said, "Yeah, I've had them flying over my head, too!"

Yet on another sunny day a neighbor drove up to my front door. He got out of his truck. He closed within 12 inches from my face and yelled. He demanded that I get rid of the homeless people on our property, or he would hang them and me, too. This was no idle threat. People have been found dead, hanging on a tree or shot by their neighbors, in this our Samaria.

I ran into a situation where Child Protective Services arrived to take children away. Three armed sheriff's deputies joined CPS, having raced to the property, sirens blaring. Inside a tent structure a family with children huddled in fear. I knew all the parties involved. A neighbor had reported the man inside the structure of menacing with a gun. I knew the accused had guns. I walked inside to size up the situation and to find the family who lived there. Over the next hour I carried messages between the CPS workers, the sheriffs, and the family. Fortunately, the conflict ended peacefully.

One day I received a phone call from a church member who lived across the highway telling me a fire blazed at the hippie camp up the street. I saw the flume of smoke and raced there. I encountered twenty-five neighbors standing around watching the fire erupt. I asked the crowd if anyone had checked to see if there were people inside the fence. Nobody knew. They watched and did not help because they hated these homeless people who came to our church. I ran through the open tin fence gate and woke the people up. I remain amazed at the crowd's heartlessness.

A couple who originally came to us homeless, then moved

into town had not been heard from for a few weeks. I checked with the clinic to see if they had appeared for their appointments. None of our church members had talked with them. Nobody had seen or heard from them in a few weeks. So, I drove out to the family house where they were staying, and where we had married them. I knocked on the door and nobody answered. A stack of mail lay on the step. Something didn't feel right. I walked around the house and checked other doors and windows. I noticed flies inside the window of a bedroom and a putrid smell emanating from the house. I didn't like how this looked. I made a few calls and the sheriff deputies came out. They broke open the door and discovered the couple dead from a murder-suicide. This discovery was as shocking as it was sad to us.

All of this ministry has to be done with grace. Amazing Grace.

THE CALL

Are these the types of issues you think a church pastor deals with? If your vision of church fits the opening paragraph, then no, it isn't. Most pastors do not experience these because they are not Living Among Them. They are in that peaceful castle safely separated. Those of you who are willing to wade into the world of the unchurched—this is the life you will experience.

What did Jesus do? He most certainly waded into the life of the common folk who lived outside the walls of Jerusalem.

Put your waders on and let's go!

CHAPTER 2

Live Among Them

- Described
- The Principle
- Is It For Me?
- Jesus Did It
- Could You Do It?

DESCRIBED

Live Among Them is a timeless principle I picked up some-where along the line and followed intuitively. This theme has been used as a basis for many a story or movie plot. Some people find this approach to be scary, others have no interest, but I find it exciting. So much so, that when I go on vacation I want to experience the daily life of those who live where I'm visiting, rather than do the touristy things like parasailing or zip-lining. I want to stay at their house or in their in-law quarters out back rather than a hotel so that I can experience their lives.

Living Among Them is what we read in the Acts of the Apostles, the Gospels, and Paul's letters to the churches. This is also known as "walking a mile in their shoes"—seeing what life looks like from their perspective. Walk with them through life, at least for a short time. Through this we develop a relational connection and build relationships for Jesus.

Live Among Them could be simply described as literally residing in the community we are ministering to. Our house is there. We are involved in the things that the community does. We go to their grocery store and post office. Our car mechanic lives there. Our kids play in the park with their children. We eat at the same restaurants they do. We cross paths with people of that community every week. They come to our house to borrow things or we go to their house to borrow something. When they need help, we are right there. When they need a referral to someone, they call us. If someone in the community dies, we are there comforting them or bringing them food. We are shoulder to shoulder with them. This is in contrast to living in a community, traveling to another community for ministry, only to return home to your community at the end of the day.

THE PRINCIPLE

The principle of Live Among Them is key to making disciples. Living in their midst helps us have a frame of reference. Jesus' parables used everyday examples to communicate a spiritual lesson. He knew the people, knew what they thought, knew what they had to deal with in their daily life. Many people do not want to be discipled, or counseled by someone who hasn't had to deal with the same things. An alcoholic finds most help from a recovered alcoholic.

A common understanding or frame of reference applies to how we conduct mission trips and how we serve our community. This frame of reference is the basis of having empathy for those to whom we minister. Some people are gifted as empathetic, but most of us have to acquire the ability somehow. Living Among Them is how we acquire a common understanding.

The apostle Paul summarized his technique for missions, evangelism, and church planting in his letter to the church in Corinth.

To the weak I became weak, that I might win the weak; I have become all things to all men, so that I may by all means save some. I do all things for the sake of the gospel, so that I may become a fellow partaker of it. 1 Corinthians 9:22-23

If we are perceived as a foreigner with no understanding, trying to convert someone to a foreign way of living and a foreign God, the hearer will often tune us out. This is not absolute. Some people love to hear and experience foreign things. We all love foreign accents. But if the foreign way comes across as condescending, we've lost their attention.

Paul also shows us that we should not be self-absorbed as we try to reach the lost. We should be concerned enough for them that we would be willing to sit on the ground with the sign-hangar on the corner, or not be aghast when we visit someone living in a filthy shack. Walk right in and sit down. Ignore the surroundings. Talk to them about them. I know some of you are feeling like vomiting just thinking about walking into the junkyard they call home and talking to them like nothing is off. If you comment, find something intriguing about the old broken down junk car or tractor. Sit on that ugly couch on their porch.

This does not extend to taking up unbiblical behavior to relate to them. Don't start cussing, telling coarse jokes, watching porn with them, or getting drunk with them. We are to still be the light of Christ to them. Find ways to give them hope. Let Christian love radiate from you.

IS IT FOR ME?

You would be right in asking yourself, "Is this method of ministry for me? Am I cut out for this?" The reality is that Live Among Them is intense. Ministering this way is not a walk in the park. You will be afflicted and persecuted. You will hear things from people that you truly don't want to hear. Your innocence will be gone. On the flip side, you will feel like you are a part of the book of Acts going into communities that seem devoid of any Christian influence and living out the gospel. You will pray more because you desperately need the encouragement.

If you aren't willing to put other's needs ahead of yours—you might hold off. If you are the type that views the world based on how you benefit, consider a supporting role while your worldview adjusts. If you are considering this ministry wondering how you will benefit, here's the answer—not much. You are certain to lose sleep. You will suffer trials and persecution. The privilege will cost you financially. You are unlikely to win an award. Therefore, the focus has to be what the ministry of Jesus will do for others. However, your church will grow in maturity and knowledge. The suffering will refine your congregation. Over time you will notice a difference in your community.

The basis for this type of ministry is 'doing it' for Jesus. Simply that. You must truly desire to live like an apostle in the first century.

JESUS DID IT

Consider how Jesus went to people's homes. He walked instead of being carried by an entourage. He went in and ate with them. Drank wine with them. Laughed with them. Cried with them. But in all circumstances Jesus gave thanks and gave people hope.

Maybe you didn't catch on to this principle of Living Among Them as part of Jesus' instructions when He sent the disciple out to evangelize.

Now after this the Lord appointed seventy others, and sent them in pairs ahead of Him to every city and place where He Himself was going to come. And He was saying to them, "The harvest is plentiful, but the laborers are few; therefore beseech the Lord of the harvest to send out laborers into His harvest. Go; behold, I send you out as lambs in the midst of wolves. Carry no money belt, no bag, no shoes; and greet no one on the way. Whatever house you enter, first say, 'Peace be to this house.' If a man of peace is there, your peace will rest on him; but if not, it will return to you. Stay in that house, eating and drinking what they give you; for the laborer is worthy of his wages. Do not keep moving from house to house. Whatever city you enter and they receive you, eat what is set before you; and heal those in it who are sick, and say to them, The kingdom of God has come near to you.' But whatever city you enter and they do not receive you, go out into its streets and say, 'Even the dust of your city which clings to our feet we wipe off in protest against you; yet be sure of this, that the kingdom of God has come near.' I say to you, it will be more tolerable in that day for Sodom than for that city. Luke 10:1-12

Stay in that house, eating and drinking what they give you. Live where they live, eat what they eat, drink what they drink, travel in whatever way they travel. I find this compelling and exciting at the same time. You may fear riding in an old pickup with ripped seats, wondering if the vehicle is going to break down. I pray for you that it does! Imagine the experience you'll have on the side of the road figuring out how you are going to solve the problem! And isn't that divine moment the absolute perfect time for you to demonstrate the power of God? Pray out loud for the situation and give God the credit when He answers. Ride the old crowded bus with them. Experience the delay of mass-transit. Observe their world. Walk the final mile to the destination with them.

"Car Therapy" is a divine technique of counseling and a slice of Living Among Them. Giving someone a ride somewhere is akin to having a captive audience. The block of time facilitates talking with them. Listening to them. To get to know them better. To counsel. I recommend you offer rides to those in need and take advantage of the captive time. Remember in Acts where Philip walked alongside a caravan and had occasion to testify to the eunuch riding inside? These opportunities come up when we are walking where they walk.

Jesus is the greatest example of Living Among Them, ever. Consider, first, that He came forth from heaven to be born among men, to live with them and die for them. He experienced humanity so that we could experience God. Secondly, He went to where people were and walked with people. This is in direct contrast to the typical king who has a palace for people to visit him. If one has a request of the king, they make an appointment and encounter him at his throne. The king does not go to the peasant's house and eat with them—heavens no!

Jesus' first miracle occurred at a wedding—an everyday event that involved a lot of people enjoying the special occasion. This opening miracle happened soon after being baptized by His cousin John, among a great crowd of people.

The first two apostles, Andrew and Simon Peter, wondered where Jesus stayed. While scripture does not describe Jesus' lodging, it appears the disciples found it both temporary and not significant enough to elaborate on. This fact underscores Jesus' main passion—people not castles. The Gospels detail our Lord's journeys by foot, up, down, and around Israel and Galilee. He walked with people, traveled in their boats with them, and borrowed a donkey to ride into Jerusalem for that final week. There are numerous stories of Him visiting with disciples and Pharisees in their homes, often sharing a meal. His meetings with spiritually curious crowds were often outside or as a guest at someone's house. Jesus picked up the twelve apostles right where they were at, usually conducting their trade. He didn't hold interviews from a castle.

Who could forget the infamous meeting with the Samaritan woman at the well? Jesus and the disciples purposely took a route that led them to that historical well. And when invited, they went into town and stayed for three days.

Jesus consistently socialized with people. He lived among them. He did not send them a scroll by messenger to be read in the public square. He went personally and spoke to them. He didn't conduct His teaching from a secluded room projecting images on a screen over the internet—a common technique for modern preachers and churches. In contrast to this, Jesus went to the beach, the mountainside, the town square, the pool sides, the Pharisee's house, the Synagogue on Saturday, and the upper rooms of houses on Sundays.

COULD YOU DO IT?

If I may, I ask you for a little tolerance of the following description of a typical American church's approach to ministry. I'd like to illustrate what the American church looks like to unchurched people. I am not making a judgment or saying all churches need to be a Live Among Them church.

The unchurched see a nice building located in a commercial zone, often along the main street. People can enter the building on Sunday mornings and possibly during office hours. Common protocol is that a phone call, screened by a secretary, might yield an appointment with the pastor. This is if the church has 300 or more members. For that matter, the vast majority of churches across America are small and don't even have office hours. If you drive by during the week the building is empty and the doors are locked. What are the pastor and elders doing during the week? Most likely they are either working a second job (often bi-vocational ministry is necessary), busy with meetings or in their libraries studying. Almost guaranteed that they live in a different community than where the church is located.

The typical weekday ministry event is held in that church building at times convenient to the working class. Bible studies are often just a one-hour open and closed session for those who are part of that group. In this day and age, once the invited group is gathered, the doors are locked or a security guard is on duty. The church may be overly worried about keeping the building clean, tidy, and organized. They can be obsessive about making sure things aren't stolen. They sometimes erroneously believe the building and contents belong to them and "if the needy need something they should look elsewhere." Jesus did not have a guarded and locked truck following Him around with all of His possessions. Most church food pantries are called food banks. They store their food and sparingly give to the needy who come at the appointed time, sign in, show their papers, and stand in line. "Preferably outside, thank you."

As stated earlier, not all churches are called to be the Live Among Them type. But if yours is, you might see if any of the above characteristics need to be changed.

A typical mission trip is organized in such a way that the church and members' standard of life is preserved. A nice church van is commandeered, everyone has a bottle of water, lunch is brought along or a restaurant is reserved. If the trip is out of town or country, a nice hotel is chosen for home base. Missionaries are taught how to keep from picking up germs or diseases from those they minister to: gloves, masks, antibacterial gel, social distancing. And to reward everyone for their sacrificial service, an event is planned in the evening at the hotel. This might include sharing stories from the day. The evening will most certainly include a nice catered meal followed by swim time or movie time. Oh, and make sure none of "those people" follow you back to the hotel. Again, I'm sorry to be so curt, but this is what the indigenous people experience from the American missionaries.

The Live Among Them principle doesn't mean a church should not have a building or desire to keep their church neat and tidy, nor that the pastor should not have private study time. The principle does not preclude going on a foreign mission trip. The challenge is to think strategically about where we locate the building and how we minister to those we live among. We should recognize that the building and the contents belong to Jesus for use in a manner that brings people to Him. If something is stolen or broken, that becomes an issue between that person and Jesus. The principle is a guide for how we do mission trips as well as daily ministry. We become like them in order to relate and expose Jesus to them. This is not to say we become an alcoholic to minister to an alcoholic, but we acknowledge our weaknesses as we build our relationship with them.

At this point you are hopefully asking how you can Live Among Them. If we use Paul's statement from 1 Corinthians 9:22-23 above, we can identify a few of the basics. Don't move into an area with low median income and drive a new Mercedes. Buy a car below your economic ability. Drive an old car that is likely to break down and need repairs. Why?

Because that's what your community deals with in their daily life. When you have to find a good mechanic, you will be asking for a referral. You'll be going to the same mechanic they do. Don't buy or build the biggest luxurious house in the neighborhood. Live below your means and similar to the level your congregation does. Dress like they dress. You will be perceived as more approachable. Use all the money you've saved in these three areas alone to help others in the community.

If your only choice of neighborhood for your church is a wealthy one, you are going to have to figure out how to fit in and yet be an example. You won't likely be able to match their opulent living, but maybe close enough so that they feel you are one of them. Look for a common point of connection. Living among the upwardly mobile is a delicate balance; living like the Jones' but not in debt like they are. Try to set an example on how to use one's wealth for the good of others rather than oneself. You will be living a notch or two below them, yet simultaneously trying to elevate their humility and Jesus-purposed way of living.

Can you do this? Yes! By God's grace.

Let's journey through the following chapters and see if and how this might transform your ministry and life!

CHAPTER 3

Foreign Mission Trips - The Jesus Way

- Experiences
- The Target
- The Draw
- The Method
- The Approach
- The Discovered Purpose

EXPERIENCES

In 1997, a stay-at-home dad, I looked for a way to do ministry. The internet came into our lives. One day I opened the instruction manual for a modem I had ordered to install in my computer and get on the internet. Reading the instructions is not my norm. However, being intrigued with the chapter describing how HTML (hypertext markup language) could be displayed on web browsers—I experimented with coding and made my own website. Soon after, I offered free websites to churches.

You can imagine my surprise when the first four requests I received came from Uganda. Africa. What? I didn't know anyone from Africa. My extent of knowledge consisted of National Geographic shows and magazines. For the next five years I created 150+ websites for churches throughout Africa, not just Uganda. Every church invited me to visit them. I felt like the year 2000 would be the time to go. I had no idea how mission trips were done. In faith, I set a date about nine months out.

Every month leading up to that date, I learned something about mission trips. Apparently, I was clueless. Missionaries were to be sent by or with an organization who had training as an evangelist or a pastor, not a computer nerd like me. In spite of my naiveté, clothing for children and books and Bibles were gathered up to give out in Uganda. Fortunately, Uganda proved very easy enter. One could pay for the visa upon landing as Customs was pretty low-key. Miraculously, they didn't collect any tax-duty from me! I had suitcases full of clothing, toys, and computers.

I landed and exited the small bullet-ridden airport building. About 30 Africans greeted me. I was the only white guy in sight. The sky grew dark as I approached a car. I opened the passenger door, or so I thought, and to my surprise—a steering wheel! We laughed and I switched sides. We drove through very small villages on narrow roads for about an hour, then arrived at the place they arranged for me to stay. We entered a small concrete house with bars on the window, situated in a compound with a handful of other small concrete houses, and a shared dirt lot. We sat around in the house's large room and talked, prayed, and worshipped, before being directed to the room prepared for me to stay in. I would soon get quite an awakening on African kitchens and bathrooms.

My guiding principle, simply, "to stay where they stay, travel how they travel, go where they go, eat what they eat, and drink what they drink." Shouldn't be too hard.

Over the next four weeks I traveled around Ugandan towns, into the far reaches of the rural areas, and across borders into other countries. I joined the people walking into the bush to fill up jugs of water for household use. I visited local hospitals and villages to pray for people dying of AIDS. I attended their churches and outdoor conferences and revivals. I participated in their funerals and weddings. I visited their children's schools as a guest speaker. I even stayed at orphanages. I used the internet cafes where everyone accessed their email. Needless to say, life was different here than at home.

During the week I conducted high tech seminars for pastors. A group gathered in an internet cafe or a school room where we arranged to have a computer for everyone. I thought I'd be teaching them how to make websites for their ministries. But when you bring people in from the village with no electricity or computers, one must start at the beginning. "Here is the ON switch. The internet is a series of computers all around the world connected by phone lines".

THE TARGET

The target is the object we are aiming at. In ministry that target is a community or a person. We put that target in our sight. We look at it. We pray while we focus in. We then set off toward the object of our focus.

Jesus tells us to go and make disciples. He tells us to be His witnesses in Jerusalem, Judea, Samaria, and the remote parts of the earth. Therefore, foreign mission trips will always be in the picture. The Bible does not give us step-by-step methods of disciple-making or how to do a mission trip. However, if we follow the lead of Jesus and Paul, we discover disciple-making means we must be among the people where they are. Usually, travel to other places than where we live, will be required.

Foreign mission trips are a very practical training ground for us to learn the principle of Live Among Them. We can choose to stay where they stay, travel how they travel, go where they go, eat what they eat, and drink what they drink. I find it so sad to see missionaries traveling in a chartered bus, bringing their own water and food, and staying in an expensive hotel or a segregated mission house, there but not among.

The fruit from these early mission trips astounded me. True miracles occurred. Small African or Indian village churches were discovered by people in the industrialized world. Donations and missionaries flowed in. Many of these pastors traveled to America and met with churches later became supporters.

THE DRAW

Conducting foreign mission trips in this Live Among Them manner engaged the indigenous people. This unique approach drew them to me. Even though I was entirely different in culture and appearance, my participation in their lives moved them to embrace me. They knew they could invite me to their house or church. I sat inside their mud huts on the dirt floor and talked with them. They made me part of their activity or group. I walked dirt trails miles back into the jungle and sat with widows on the ground or on a makeshift bench. I ate their food. I played soccer with their children. I tried my best to keep up with a young pastor as we ran from his village to the road a few miles away. At the end of the day I returned with the native ministers and hosts and stayed at their places, rather than separate and go to a hotel or mission compound with all of its conveniences.

THE METHOD

Living Among Them is a very simple method of ministry —stay where they stay, travel how they travel, go where they go, eat what they eat, and drink what they drink. I told them as long as they ate or drank something first, I would follow suit. This advice is simple to hear, but for many, *very* hard to do. This approach requires us to give up convenience, often requiring us to try something new.

Developing country's kitchens are nothing like Western kitchens. Their kitchens are not laid out with upper and lower cabinets, nice countertops, sinks and disposals, built-in dishwashers and electric outlets. Rarely is there a refrigerator. This means no ice-cream or popsicles, or ice in your drinks. Their kitchens resemble an open food pantry in a campsite. The area is stocked with large plastic bowls containing bulk-food items and burlap bags with root foods. The cooking is frequently done with charcoal or wood in a basic outdoor grill, or literally in an outdoor makeshift room attached to the back of the house.

Imagine my shock the first time going to the bathroom to find just a hole in the floor! Not even a bench with a hole to sit on. Heck, even our campgrounds have that! But not there. The technique is squatting above a hole in the floor. After finishing my business I reached for the toilet paper. There wasn't any. The little pitcher of water and bar of soap they gave me was for personal hygiene. Could you do it?

Right after the tsunami that hit the shores of India in 2005, I went to stay with a rural pastor in Rajahmundry. While there we drove through busy streets in 3-wheeled vehicles. You haven't experienced near-death until you ride in one! Drivers speed head-on toward another vehicle and turn at the last second. Once, we were stuck in a traffic jam with a huge dump truck, its wheel as tall as our vehicle just inches away. The driver attempted to push his way through the jam. I thought for sure we were going to be run over. Continuing on, we traveled miles out to a pastors' conference in a village on the ocean. We spent all day preaching and teaching in a single room thatch building with concrete floor. After dinner we prepared to retire. Right there on the concrete floor. All 40 of us. Lined up next to each other. Wasn't sure I could do it. When I go camping I always have a sleeping pad underneath me. Well you heard me say, stay where they stay. That was quite an experience.

In Africa, a scooter or moped is considered a luxury. You frequently see a family of 5 riding one—all at the same time. I rode on the back of those things all around Africa and India. They are pretty handy in traffic jams.

Another common mode of African transport is vans. They have bus parks in the middle of town which are huge dirt lots with dozens and dozens of vans and busses jammed together. Somehow people find the one that is driving the needed route. I have no idea how they know. There are no signs. Everyone climbs in the 12 passenger Toyota van through the sliding door. After the twelfth person boards, you figure, okay, time to shut the door and go. Oh no. There's room for at least 4-5 more people. Then you close the door and go. If you are catching the van in the streets you run alongside and jump in —while it's moving. One of the two man team operating the van is responsible for getting people in and out and collecting the fare. How he knows who has paid and who hasn't is a mystery to me. He doesn't collect money as you board. Fares are handed over sometime later while you are moving. With so many people seated inside and that many more getting on or off, keeping track of the fares is quite the talent. Traveling this way is truly getting close with the people.

The busses travel cross-country down roads pocked with pothole after pothole. The luxury busses are a little nicer, but still very basic. At various points in time, the bus pulls over to the side of the rural road and everyone piles out...to go to the bathroom on the side of the road! Wow. Riders cannot ask the driver to stop. They only stop for everyone, occasionally. I can remember times that African pastors have visited me in the USA and had me stop my car while they attempted to go to the bathroom right there in public.

One time, while in Africa, a couple of preteen boys took me to task. Wearing devious smiles, they scooped up a termite from a mound on the ground—and ate it! I did the same. Picked one up and tossed the critter into my mouth. Come to think of it, I never did see the termite actually go into their mouths. Hmmm...

Another time I rode in a car with a pastor and his family. Booths along the street sold all manner of food and trinkets. The driver stopped at a stand selling cooked carcasses on sticks neatly lined up on a table. He rolled down the car window, gave the merchant some money, and received a carcass in return. You guessed it. We ate it. They were called grass cutters. Later on I saw these furry gopher-looking animals being raised for food in rabbit hutches. Wait a minute....

I've walked back into in the jungle to a widow's mud and straw hut. She sat outside in the dirt sorting out grain in a basket. She was so poor. I sat with her and visited. I shared Jesus with her through my translators. When I got ready to leave she asked me to wait. This precious lady caught one of her few chickens and gave the catch to me as a thank you gift. I carried the flopping bird upside down by the legs all the way back to the village. When came dinner time the cooks had me chop the head off! They were kind enough to do the plucking. We had fresh chicken for dinner. Thank you Jesus.

THE APPROACH

Living Among Them on a mission trip will draw people to you. This approach is a fairly unusual way for mission trips to be structured. Indigenous people are intrigued by foreigners. They want to get to know them, hear their accents, and even just touch their skin or hair. They want to hear about what life is back home. They are curious to learn if there are any commonalities.

There is much fruit to be gained from this approach. Spending time with someone allows the gospel to be lived out and weaved into conversations. Quick friendships are born.

THE DISCOVERED PURPOSE

The discovered purpose for me, after a dozen mission trips in several countries, became this principle of Live Among Them. The principle carried on in me as I entered into full-time ministry and planted churches. During the first mission trip I mentioned earlier, I felt called into ministry as a pastor. Later, upon being called by God to plant a church, my wife, Jesus, and I knew we needed to buy a house in the neighborhood of the community where we would plant the church. In fact, we started the church in the house.

Anytime someone moves into a rural area, they are not considered to be a local right away. Acceptance can take years. People wait to see if you ascribe to their culture and way of thinking or if you are bringing in foreign ways to replace what is familiar. Of course, we do move in to change the spiritual landscape, else we wouldn't be moving in. However, if we use the Live Among Them principle, we blend in and are accepted more quickly.

We are ambassadors of Heaven. Let our purpose be in exposing Jesus to the world.

CHAPTER 4

Be Ready With Your Testimony

- God Shapes Us
- God Uses Our Personality and Skills
- The Primary Necessity
- I Know My Past
- Be Ready with Your Testimony

GOD SHAPES US

God shapes us through our life experiences in a purposeful way. I would venture to say that this observation is only made in hind-sight. Few of us would think, "Oh, God is doing this in my life to shape me for ministry in the future." In fact, this makes sense. God's interaction in our life is redemptive. We've failed or made a mess of things and He redeems us, or simply unfolds a way to use the mess for divine purpose.

The Bible is full of stories about the failures and victories of humans and how God used those people. There is always growth in their character. Those who don't grow come to a less than inspiring end. King David is a classic case of the ups and downs of obedience to God, but God said that he was a man after God's heart. He used David's son, Solomon, in dramatic fashion for the revelation of His character. King Saul started out well, but ended miserably, committing suicide during battle. Eli, the priest, came to an ignoble end due to poor oversight and parenting of his two carnal sons. Who could not be inspired by the rags-to-riches stories of Ruth and Esther? Job went from miraculous blessing, to the deepest depths, back to restored heights. Jesus picked men to be apostles right from their secular vocations. He knew their character before He called them. After Jesus left them and returned to Heaven, He left the ministry of the gospel in their hands. One of the more dramatic life transitions in the New Testament is that of Saul. The Saul that became the Apostle Paul. He is known to us as a renowned evangelist, a prolific church planter, and author of half of the New Testament.

God shaped me, took my sin-directed life and repurposed it to be used by Him and for Him. He picked me up from the mire and set me on a new path. My whole life has been redirected to serving Him in serving others. And my life couldn't be more exciting!

GOD USES OUR PERSONALITY AND SKILLS

God uses our innate personality and skills. This shouldn't be too surprising as He is the One who created us. Created us down to our DNA. Gave us our personality, our looks, even the parents to whom we were born. He chose where we would be born and what time in history we'd exist. Those life-stories mentioned in the previous paragraph are a testimony to this sovereign action of God. Does the same principle apply to us? Unquestionably. God can use the meekest or the most arrogant person for His grand purposes. He chose the young Mary to bear His only begotten Son. He used the pagan Nebuchadnezzar to discipline His chosen nation, Israel. This king once walked on his roof declaring himself the greatest. Not much later God confined this king to crawling around eating grass, only to be restored and declare that Daniel's God is the only true God.

The Apostle Paul teaches us through his letter to the church in Corinth, that each of us is a part of the body of Christ. Just a part, not the whole. Not everyone is the same part. We are each a unique part. We bring to the body our innate personality, skills, experiences, and spiritual gifts. While in college, my greatest contribution was organizing parties and inviting people to them. I planned them every week. I spent my time each day inviting people to the upcoming kegger. Now you may ask, how can God use this skill? Think church planter, evangelist, and pastor. Aren't these all needed skills? Yes.

I grew up as a military brat. Our family moved about every two years. I attended new schools and had to make a whole set of new friends. I went door-to-door in my new neighborhood to see who had kids I could play with. For real! I also became renowned for door-to-door fundraising in my Boy Scout troop. Can you see how God could use these talents for His kingdom?

What about you? What traits, skills, or experiences do you have that can be translated into ministry efforts? Take some time to identify them as they are, then overlay them on ministry possibilities. Spiritual Gift Assessments can be of help for this exercise.

THE PRIMARY NECESSITY

Willingness is the prime ingredient to being used by and for Jesus. The right answer is, "Send me, I will go." The prophet Isaiah had a vision one day of heaven wherein he heard the Lord asking, "Whom shall I send?" Isaiah cried out, "Here am I. Send me!"

Referring once again to Saul (Paul), God can do things in our life to give us that willingness we might be lacking. On the road to Damascus, a bright light blinded Saul such that he had to be led by the hand to one of God's people who prayed for him. He received his sight back after three days. Saul, filled with the Holy Spirit and baptized, was now ready to go! In similar manner, I had to be slapped to the pavement before I would finally listen and turn around.

I think the seed of willingness is acquired through prayer. While praying we can have "Isaiah" visions or simply hear God telling us to get ready and go. I remember riding my bike home from work one day, a couple years into my marriage. I sat on my bicycle waiting for traffic to pass before turning up my street. I said to God, "I will go wherever you want me to go. I want to do that Lord." Little did I know that I had to go through some significant pain before that would come about.

The infamous prophet and evangelist Jonah heard a

command from God, but refused to obey. He was not willing. Maybe you do this as well? You've heard God tell you to do something, but you just refuse. Jonah had to go through some pain and get swallowed by a big fish before he had the willingness to go. Then he was only too happy to pray and go.

I find that many long-time Christians say they are "resting in the Lord" waiting for Him to give them the command or direction. Truth be known, they are just delaying. God wants those who are willing to step out in faith. These "resters" would not even go if God sent them a brand new RV. They'd be inside the RV playing with the electronics and "resting" until a map appeared and the autonomous driving started the journey. If this is you, I apologize for being so blunt. There are biblical ways and times for us to rest in the Lord. Let's aim to rest in the right way. Proper "resting in the Lord" is actively seeking a direction and having the true motive of going once you hear. The question is not "if", but rather, "when, where, who, how?" More of the specifics. He has already told us in the Bible to go and do. Let us not be found postponing.

You are probably reading this book because you either don't have that willingness to Live Among Them yet, or you do have the desire, but don't know the "how". Spend time in prayer. Time alone with God. Time with your eyes closed and letting those visions come to you. Seek His face on this. While you are traveling going through the grocery store, have your spiritual thoughts set on this. Be receptive to how God wants to answer. Have your ears open. Have your eyes open and assess things from a spiritual standpoint. Read your Bible reflectively. See if God provides the willingness through His word penetrating your heart. You don't have to be slammed to the pavement like me, or blinded like Saul, or swallowed by a fish like Jonah, to get the message for heaven's sake. Don't insist on having everything revealed or planned out for you. Get the direction and start out in faith. God will reveal what needs to be revealed in His perfect timing. We live out the assignment as we go, taking each step in its time.

I KNOW MY PAST

You might also be thinking you aren't qualified, or even worse—disqualified. I said to an African pastor, while sitting in his house after service, "I feel like I'm being called into ministry. But, I know my past. I haven't gone to seminary. I can't see how I could be a pastor."

What was my past you ask?

I grew up in a church-going, Christian home. We were at church multiple times a week—attending youth group, Boy Scouts, choir practice, and church service every Sunday. We served as acolytes and as laborers when they were building a new church. You get the picture. In all of this training, I never truly caught on that salvation is about a relationship with Jesus.

In our teenage years, my 4 brothers and I would sneak out at night and party or visit our girlfriends. We'd make the dummies in bed to fool our parents. Our Mom made hats and kept those head molds in our closet. We made great use of them for our dummies. After we left home for college, we quit going to church and, as stated earlier, became party organizers. I spent 15 years committing every sin possible. I am and was so embarrassed before God over the things I did and the people I hurt. I was such a tool of Satan.

At age 30 I crashed my motorcycle while driving drunk on Super Bowl Sunday. I don't even remember the accident. I woke up in the hospital a few days later. I was drinking at a bar and should have been in church. The motorcycle was all I owned and now, even that was broken. I remember walking down the street and telling God out loud, "I know I haven't been living like you want me to." I determined to go back to church and live my life every day doing the will of God. Now I was willing. I went to church that Easter and began crying in the service. I heard "Welcome home." I'm not sure if the pastor was saying that or Jesus talking to me, but I heard the message. That summer I crutched my way to the church across the street from my office, which had been my home for the last few months. I gave my life to Jesus. I asked Him to give me a wife I didn't find in a bar. A year and half later I met my wife of 30 years at a Ski Bunk and Breakfast in the mountains. Thank you Jesus.

I didn't have a driver's license for the first seven years of our marriage. During this time we had two very small, preemie children. I had to close my business so that both of us could care for them round the clock during the first six months of our second-born's life. About this time, my wife and I prayed for a job with benefits and whomever received a job offer would go to work. Adrienne applied to the County of Sacramento three years prior. She got an offer the very day her application would have expired! We had given up hope on that job. She accepted the job and we knew this blessing was a divine moment in our life.

Meanwhile, under investigation by the FBI, I accepted a plea bargain and had to spend six months under house arrest and pay a fine of $40,000. This marked the beginning of being the house dad and homeschool dad, soon after that bicycle ride home I mentioned earlier. During this at-home period I learned how to create websites and started on that journey of creating church websites. You see, my circumstances did not stop my willingness to serve God. The legal consequences shaped my heart. They redirected me into what God would use several years down the road—that date of saying to God, "Yes, I'll go to Africa on a mission trip."

By the time I started mission trips, Adrienne had a job working for the State of California. We were living in the small town of Bishop, California and still homeschooling our children, now in fifth and sixth grade. Leaving my wife and children at home was not easy on us. Adrienne had to somehow figure out how to work, homeschool our kids, and be Mom and Dad—for four weeks. Her willingness to say "Yes" to Jesus made it possible for me to go. Even those who helped her during my absence were saying "Yes" to Jesus. Do you see how there are so many ways you can serve God without necessarily being on the front lines? I hope so.

BE READY WITH YOUR TESTIMONY

Be ready with your testimony. You just read mine. Our testimony is integral to how people might believe that they too can be saved. After all, if God can "save you, surely He can save me". People will find a point of connection to your testimony. Your testimony should be ready to be spoken at any instant. Many people feel like a testimony isn't important. Wrong. Non-believers or the not-willing need to hear how Jesus worked in your life before they can understand the real-world spiritual actions of the Holy Spirit. Maybe you don't feel comfortable talking about yourself. To be sure, your testimony isn't really about you—it's about Jesus.

Be ready with your testimony. Prepare one. Write it out. Practice speaking the testimony. The more you share the message, the easier the words will flow. A few practical guidelines for your testimony: Keep it short. Just a few minutes, not 10-20 minutes. This will increase the effectiveness rather than being a "turn-off". Of course, you have to hold some of the story back in case they ask questions. Hopefully they will! Start with a description of your life before Jesus. Identify the point when you realized you needed Him. Describe the moment you surrendered and how being born-again has impacted you. Finish with what Jesus means to you and what He's done in your life. If you haven't been water baptized— now's the time. The Holy Spirit works through that event and that person who stands before others declaring Jesus as Lord.

Can I get a witness?

CHAPTER 5

Domestic Outdoor Church Plant

- Go Where They Are
- Resistance by Idolaters and Government
- Disasters along the Way
- Use What You Have

GO WHERE THEY ARE

This chapter is how Live Among Them collided with *willingness* and *God using our personality* in my life. This collision took place over four years beginning in 2002 and blossoming in 2006. Adrienne and I had been married about 10 years when this part of the story started. Our two children were eight and nine and homeschooled. We moved to Bishop, California after having lived in Folsom, California for about 9 years (yeah, where the prison is). Folsom is where we were living when I said yes to Jesus about going on a mission trip. To...*go where they are*.

After that mission trip to Uganda, I came home asking why we Americans couldn't do church like the Africans. Wouldn't that be exciting? We were attending a Baptist church at the time. I asked one of the pastors about doing things that would bring in the unchurched, including a second service on Saturday night with contemporary music. The enthusiastic request went over like a lead balloon. My wife and I learned from a precious old lady at that church, "Baptists don't dance, they don't play cards, or go to movies."

The pastor from Uganda came to visit us in our home. Wow, that was exciting and the beginning of hosting many a foreign pastor. I updated him on how I wanted to plant a church like the ones I saw popup in the street in Africa. We prayed and I decided I had the willingness. I made preparations. I sought out the vision and wrote it down. I identified to whom I would go. But before God would release us, my wife had to get baptized. She did, in a hot springs pool. Wham! The doors were opened.

We began by renting a storefront to have a church that would be visible and located where rock climbers would find us. Bishop is a world-class climbing spot, population 4500, and the weekend spot for Los Angelenos. The area is on the way to Mammoth Lakes, a world-renowned ski area. We called the church, "The Source Is." A play on words. Bishop, the source of the Owens River, fed Los Angeles with water. More importantly, Jesus is the source. We added the *is* so that people would ask what the source is. We were only too happy to answer that! Well, we got kicked out of that retail space in a few short months. Now what?

Remember "Go Where They Are?" Who are *they*? The rock climbers and city people vacationing in the mountains. Where are they? They are camping in the State Forest, National Park, and Bureau of Land Management (BLM) lands. Ok, fair enough. I love camping, backpacking, and climbing. We gathered up a musician to be our worship leader and started doing church services in the campgrounds and at the rock climbing spots. We did, really! I scouted out the campground during the week to determine where we'd set up the following Sunday. Then I'd walk site-to-site meeting people and asking if they would come to church Sunday. At times I'd even get people to let us do a midweek Bible study at their campground.

We would spend 2-3 weeks at a site, then move on to another. Variety is the spice of life, right? Maybe not for you. However, I'm sharing these things to spur ideas in you. At times, we set up near a fishing lake and aimed one of the speakers out at the lake so fishermen could be part of the service. Believe it! Every week we put a portable sign out on the highway or in the campground directing people to an "Outdoor Church Service, 10 a.m." Other times we drove out a dirt BLM road to the bouldering area and just set up church. We laid out a breakfast or lunch and others invited the climbers to join us. Many times we held church in a cow pasture, literally. We held church services by a river at a free climber's campground. That camp, nothing more than vacant bare land with dirt and gravel, facilitated climbers sleeping in their vans or tents. Campers built a common fire pit and set up slack lines to entertain themselves while not climbing. I'd go site-to-site and invite them to church. Are you seeing the "Go Where They Are?" Oh, those were such fun days.

We conducted services at a ski-resort up the highway at Mammoth Lakes. There too, we walked through the bar and cafe inviting people to church outside. One week, we were in the town of Mammoth Lakes and set up church at the California State Park amphitheater. Can you believe this? California state agencies are not known for their tolerance of Christianity. That week I went door-to-door of coffee shops, restaurants, stores. Along the way I encountered a young man who said, "Yeah! I'll come." But he also said, "Hey, can I help?" He joined me doing the invites and came to church that week as well. He stayed with us for 2 years and even started doing the meals for our church service.

After 2 1/2 years of this outdoor church, my children and I moved to Colorado. Adrienne followed out in the next couple months. We relocated to a poor, small town of 1800 people where we didn't know anyone. I had no job lined up or a house to live in. The kids and I camped in a tent while I looked for these things. I found a church meeting in a nursing home and asked if they needed a pastor. Over the next five years we held services there. The church met in a stand-alone section of the building accessible to the public. We became an integral part of that nursing home. Every Sunday morning church members wheeled people to the chapel. We helped with fundraisers for the nursing home on Halloween. We were right there for the family members visiting their loved ones. We had time to minister to the workers as well. Again, "*Go Where They Are.*"

RESISTANCE BY IDOLATERS AND GOVERNMENT

Anytime you *Go Where They Are,* you will have resistance from idolaters and the government. Just a fact. You start to wonder if you are simply a troublemaker. Take heart, you aren't. Sure, you are disturbing Satan's kingdom, but that is the only way to shake loose some of his followers and bring them into the Kingdom of Christ.

The outdoor church in California encountered a lot of resistance. You can't believe how many people have the "separation of church and state" as a shield over their heart and a weapon with which to attack. When you *Go Where They Are* you will hear the mantra—among many other negative things. Why? "I mean c'mon, we aren't forcing you to come to church...we just invited you." This is a spiritual battle. No matter how kind and nice you are being, remember who the battle is with and what your weapons are. Our battle is not against the deceived and our weapons are not angry, sharp tongues.

We had people hiding in bushes, taking pictures of us holding an [illegal?] church service on public land, not inside a church building. They would do a victory dance because they caught us. Strange, huh? We had people report us to the state. I received a call one day from the local State Ranger. He said if I didn't remove our signs and refrain from holding the church service, he would arrest me. What? Arrest me for holding a church service in a national park campground? You've got to be kidding. Nope. We were able to get Jay Sekulow's legal ministry to write a letter informing them of our right to worship. We also had the health department called on us for providing a free meal at a park. People used county planning departments to require us to get a permit, which they wouldn't grant, or to legally claim us as a nuisance and zoning problem. Be prepared for the onslaught. Just stand.

USE WHAT YOU HAVE

"Use What You Have" to go and do. Don't stay immobile because you don't have the funding or the equipment. Innovate. God will provide as you go and as you operate in His will. He will bring others to provide or help. In fact, this is the basis of Jesus' instruction to the disciples He sent out to the cities of Israel—don't take anything. He wanted them to be in need so that other people would offer help or a place to stay. He used this method to make connections for the disciples. God used lack or need to bring people to the disciples who could carry out their calling of declaring peace and the good news about the Messiah.

Many churches make the mistake of thinking they have to be fully equipped and funded. I can just hear you *organizers* and *preparers* groaning. Is our God the owner of the cattle on a thousand hills or not? Did Jesus feed the crowd with a handful of fish and bread? Didn't He bring ravens to feed the prophet Elijah? In fact, if we are too prepared or too equipped, the people we encounter will have their attention on that and not be drawn to Jesus or our message.

One day while pastoring the outdoor church, we had an idea for a popup canopy. We ordered a custom double-sized one with clear walls. Our church building. We took this tent everywhere, popped it up and held church. Much like the Israelites in the wilderness. We used a second large camping tent for the childrens' Sunday School room. We bought a camper toilet and put that gem in the bushes for our bathroom. We had folding chairs for seating and a propane heater for the winter. Make do. Be creative. We rented a storage unit for the items between Sundays.

Every week we served a meal after service. That man from the coffee shop, who joined us, put out a nicely catered meal. We didn't have electricity or a kitchen. We had to figure out what to bring and how to prepare the meal onsite. Nobody complained. We looked forward to the picnic! Free food was always a draw for the people we invited to church.

Our worship leader for this outdoor church played music as a true one-man band. He wore a guitar and had a keyboard with programmed in drums and background music or voices. We powered the system with a marine battery. One Sunday, on his way up the 4000 foot climb, to a service location in a brush dump we had been relegated to by the Forest Service, his little truck carrying the music equipment caught on fire! We saw the smoke, ran over the hill and helped rescue the equipment.

Our present church in Colorado doesn't have any musicians. We started in a campground sand pit with my wife playing chords on a keyboard while we sang along. Neither she nor I are singers! When we moved into the house we bought a large flat screen and an amplifier with speakers. We connected these to our computer and played recorded music. Ten years later we are still doing this! Use what you have.

I think the bottom line for this topic is to not let lack hold you back. Use what you have. After all, what exactly is needed to gather and worship God? Just people and the Bible.

He has made everything appropriate in its time.

CHAPTER 6

Community Church Plant in Samaria

- Wasn't Plan A
- What Is Samaria?
- God Will Have His Way
- Go to the Streets and Byways
- The Happy Camper
- Door to Door Education
- Events in the Community
- Building from Weakness

WASN'T PLAN A

Are you familiar with that phrase "Plan A or Plan B"? Likely. We all have a Plan A in mind, because that one represents our first choice. The one we want to happen or how we plan on doing something. The event or objective is most often something that isn't tested. Thus, a plan—not experience. Plan B is our second choice. This is usually what happens when Plan A doesn't work out. So often, Plan B isn't even planned—simply how we describe what actually happened and we try to pretend B was *the* plan. If you are the spontaneous type you know exactly what I mean. You thrive in this environment, also known as "winging it."

After living in our previous location in Del Norte, CO for six years we were drawn to move. Things change, life goes on. Over time, I came up with a Plan A. We'll move, we'll find a house to rent, and I'll apply for a job as a pastor at one of the many churches in this small town (larger than where we were moving from). I'll have a salary. Won't that be nice. Never had one as a pastor before. With both of us working, we can pay rent. Isn't this a great Plan A?

We started visiting churches and eventually rented a tent spot in a campground in Samaria because the commute from our home 60 miles away began to wear on us. We could not find a house to rent in the new city that wasn't more than double our current house payment. Plan B, try to buy a house. The market was really down and we thought we could buy a house at an auction or foreclosure or simply find one bargain priced. We shopped and put in several offers. We pursued the areas that looked nice and where the real estate agents directed us. We stayed out of Samaria, complying with the agents' advice. All of our offers were shot down. Moreover, none of the churches in the nice areas wanted to entertain my application for the pastoral job. What about Plan C?

WHAT IS SAMARIA?

Out of desperation we decided to look in Samaria. How bad can the area really be? Driving around the subdivision, I felt a real kinship. The area looked like a big campground that we could live in, not just go camping for a few days and then go home. One day, parked on a dirt street, I heard God say, "Plant a church here." In Samaria. No church salary. An area without city water—either haul your water or use a sulfur well. We were still camping in our tent and my wife's patience began running thin. Ok, Samaria, here we go. Miraculously, her family offered us a down payment and told us to buy a house double in price of what we were looking at. After a few attempts we found one.

What is Samaria? Samaria in the Bible is the part of the country where "those people" live. The ones nobody wants to live near. Modern Samaria for most of us would be poor people, trash and junk cars in their yard, people living in campers, an area of criminals and meth labs. The community certainly wasn't known as a good area for real estate investment. But this is where God wanted us. He proved that by providing us a nice house on 10 acres and hundreds of trees. Wow, God is so good.

A few years later we found out the sweet, believing lady across the street had been praying that a Christian would buy the vacant house, the one we bought. Little did she know that her faithful prayers would not only bring a Christian family, but a church! So when you resist going to Samaria, remember that God might be directing you there in response to someone's fervent prayers. He has divine appointments for you.

Are you holding your car wash fund raisers at the nice gas station in the expensive neighborhood because you think the rich people will donate more money? What if you held the washes in Samaria? Maybe even include some repairs, or oil changes and tire repairs. Have a dumpster ready. Have food ready. Don't do the fundraiser for what money the Samaritans will pay, rather see what God will do with a humble and generous heart. What about your park day? Do you find the nicest park or do you go to Samaria? Hold a free lunch there. Bring outdoor toys. Water sports of any kind are a big hit. Are you willing to have those "dirty urchins" come to your church? There is only one correct answer here. I have found that kids don't need all the fancy blow-up houses and slides. They are so creative. They will figure out how to play together. A large pile of dirt we brought in became the best childcare I ever put together. The pile kept the kids entertained for hours. We seeded the mound with toy trucks. Consider holding a drive for donated used bicycles beforehand and take them with you. Cheap squirt guns and buckets of water will engage them immediately. Make sure to have a sit-down discussion time to share the gospel. Pray before eating any food. Get a large sheet and do those "parachute" games. Play Duck Duck Goose. Gather up names and phone numbers throughout the day. Keep inviting them.

What is Samaria? I'd say, a rich area for the gospel to be spread.

GOD WILL HAVE HIS WAY

God will have His way. What do I mean by this? We can

make plans, but God will establish our steps. That is how we ended up in Samaria. Landing there wasn't our Plan A by any stretch. You would think that we being mature Christians and one of us a pastor to boot, we would have heard God's plan before all of the house shopping, job seeking, and time wasting. Nevertheless, God redeemed our foibles and turned our ashes into diamonds. If God wants you to Live Among Them —don't fight. If God wants you to go to Samaria—just go.

God will have His way. We try to follow business models or what other churches have done or simply what we feel would be more comfortable or successful. But can any of those plans be found in the Bible? God has given us the Bible so that we will know what His way is. As demonstrated above, I'm as guilty of this as anyone else. How do we know if we are following His way? He will confirm His will. *My* vision for the church in Samaria centered around a house church where 30 faithful people, who really loved church, came each week. That defined success to me. God's plan turned out to be that I'd meet for a couple years with seven men and my wife. Some weeks the congregation consisted of one man, my wife, son, daughter and I. Midweek Bible Study included my wife, that praying neighbor lady, and me. As we pressed to find out God's plan for us, He gradually brought more and more people. We went well past 30. The church used our entire two story house in some way. The consensus of the members became, "time to flatten out some of the land and build a church building." However, I said, "But God, we don't have any money for this." One of our church members sketched out a plan for a pole barn. Fall loomed fast upon us. I started digging holes for the foundation piers. Money started coming in from outside the church. I kept digging, pouring cement, acquiring wood, erecting beams and posts nearly every day through the winter. Neighbors would come volunteer time and help. People who had to do court ordered or food stamp community service came and helped. Homeless and the poor who came by asking for money volunteered time and we helped them with gas or food, a tent or a place to camp.

Live Among Them. Rural mountain people in the low income bracket absolutely love meeting in barns and garages for anything. These settings are where they are comfortable. They'll hang out and talk tools and drink beer. By the next Fall, we stopped meeting in the house and moved into the partially constructed barn. We sat on hay bales for service and made a breakfast table out of a piece of plywood supported by sawhorses. The windows and doors were not installed yet. Plywood covered a portion of the exterior walls and the bathrooms were port-a-pottys. Heat was provided by portable propane heaters. Would you have done this? Are you willing to get out of God's way? To use what you have?

GO TO THE STREETS AND BYWAYS

If you are going to Live Among Them you should be familiar with Jesus' teaching on the Wedding Feast. The master planned a great banquet and invited people in advance. When time came to eat, the invited guests weren't there. So the master told the servants to go out into the streets and byways and bring uninvited people in. "Those people" that nobody would invite. Samaritans. The "least of these." There are a few principles to be learned here. First, inviting the "right kind of people" because of how they make you look or what they can do for you, is probably not His will. Second, don't just sit there waiting for the invited to come. Don't close up if they don't show up. Go out and compel them to come in. Make them feel welcome. Keep a careful eye out for your church or ministry plans that focus on the "right people" and not "those people." We aren't here to build our own kingdom. We're here to help Jesus build His kingdom. Jesus emphatically showed us His love for the poor in spirit and not the privileged or the self-righteous. Too many church business plans are laid out around the nice neighborhoods that are growing and how they can help the church.

If your church ministers to alcoholics and drug addicts, go to the streets and parks and compel them to come in. I had so much fun driving around the state and doing this. To this day, I hear from those who have been released from prison, who met someone inside, that knew me.

THE HAPPY CAMPER

Happy Camper. This is an everyday phrase. Also the name of the campground in Samaria where we were tenting while looking for a house. God is so great. One day while talking to the resident owner he invited me to their deck party that night. I had no interest in drinking or smoking pot but I figured I'd go anyway. While at that party he asked what I was doing in this city. I told him we were here to plant a church but were still waiting on a house. He said, "Hey, you can start one right here!' All I needed. That weekend we set up an "outdoor church" in the sand pit by the creek under a beautiful tree. We arranged to have food and we found some chairs. We put up flyers around town. I went from camper to camper and invited people to church. We held services there for about 6 weeks until we moved into our house. One of the campers still comes to church 10 years later. We stay in contact with people from those early days who moved away. Those seven men that came to church at our house came out of this campground. Some were seasonal workers. We still minister to people living there. We have present members that moved into that campground. We deliver food to other campers there. In the Sheep Barn, our church building, we have the stick cross that we fashioned for that first campground service. We used twine to hold it together and stuck the homemade cross in the sand. We found the sticks in the creek. Note that we were living in a two man tent about 50 feet from this outdoor church. Do you see the "Live Among Them," "Use What You Have," "Wasn't Plan A," principles at work here?

DOOR-TO-DOOR EDUCATION

That's door-to-door education, not evangelism or sales. Once we moved into our house, my education began when I started going door to door, inviting people to the new church. Most people were friendly enough. Some said they would come. Some just found a new church to be interesting news. Others found my visit as an opportunity to express their anger at the church and God. Some would slam the door. Others wouldn't even come to the door. They saw me walking up the drive with my big fat study Bible and knew why I was coming. Occasionally I would be invited in. I went in.

Through these encounters I found out the things in life that were important to the local people. I changed my approach. I started out by asking what their spiritual beliefs were. Even when I didn't ask, they told me. I gave them a chance to take the stage and I listened. Twenty minutes, thirty minutes. Eventually they'd ask why I came.

So here's the lesson. How often do we ask and then listen? Truth be known, almost never. Sure we might ask, but we don't listen. We might listen if they interrupt, but we look for opportunity to take over the conversation and talk about our stuff. In sales, I learned to ask people questions first and let them talk. If you listen, they will tell you what they want and how to sell the product or service to them. Spiritual matters are the same. Ask them to talk. Listen. Then ask questions. Jesus demonstrated mastery at this. He'd listen and then speak to their heart about what they actually wanted to know.

Door to Door Education. If you are Living Among Them, go and ask questions. Learn from them.

EVENTS IN THE COMMUNITY

Events in the Community—notice I said in, not for. Hold your event in the community. Don't hold church activities outside the community and expect people to leave their neighborhood to attend. This isn't absolute, more an admonition to change direction a little bit. Not all events will work in the community. Sometimes they *do* want to leave their community.

Given that you are Living Among Them have some idea what events to hold. We did a Free Lunch Saturday every Saturday during the summer. We reserved the gazebo in our community park and barbecued meat. We provided the meat, drinks, dishes and utensils. We advertised for people to bring a side dish. We didn't program anything. We simply offered the event as a time for people to visit and play. We didn't post the name of the church and we didn't preach. We had great times and gained many new members from that. We've held spontaneous play days there. We've hosted pre-planned Halloween events there. We held portions of our Vacation Summer Camp there. Tip: Remember to collect names and numbers for future invites.

We've held clean-up days in the community. Prior to the day, we invited all of the neighbors of the place we arranged to clean up and asked them to help. We posted invitation flyers as well. These types of events bring people together. If you focus your ministry events in your well-to-do neighborhood or leave your area to hold an event in the Samaria community, you begin to see the foreign nature of this approach from the perspective of the locals. People say they don't want charity. But they are much more likely to accept help from a neighbor. Charity has a different feel. Neighbors are more likely to volunteer to help you in their community rather than yours.

BUILDING FROM WEAKNESS

Paul stated the power of weakness. When we are weak, God is strong. Consider this, if our group comes from outside the community to hold an event or do a project and we have everything we need—what is there to do for neighbors or volunteers? We've robbed their opportunity! Let them provide something. Maybe a tool, a technique, some knowledge, a vehicle, materials, labor, anything. Let them shine. Even if you have to step back and let them take the lead. Don't be a know-it-all. Be weak. Be second. Let them shine. Give them the accolades. Paul wasn't weak but he became weak so that he could reach the weak. We might even unknowingly embarrass or shame the locals with our new fancy trucks and all the tools needed. Bad, bad. Serve down-home food or cook hot dogs for lunch; don't pull out the expensive catered food.

Keep an eye on your purpose. To win some over. To love and serve. This is humility. And God gives a greater grace to the humble.

CHAPTER 7

Really Live Among Them

- No Guarantees
- Conflicts and Threats
- No Good Deed Goes Unpunished
- Serve Them Anyway
- Stay Beyond the Argument
- Switching Hats

NO GUARANTEES

While the principle of Live Among Them is compelling and worthwhile, it isn't a guarantee of success or growing a large thriving church. Part of the equation is how we define success. The other part is managing our expectations of what the goal of the church is. Like any equation, these two parts combine into an answer.

I've come to understand that my purpose in life is to be a

catalyst of grace in peoples' lives. Success for me is seeing the switch from legalistic achievement to grace as the Christian's motivation. Success isn't a perfectly behaved and groomed Believer with all the boxes checked. Unfortunately, the American church has created a stereotype of the Christian life and this is what the world sees when they think of a Christian. Trying to live up to a stereotype will cause spin-out as the Believer tries to fit that mold.

We've also got to come to grips with our expectations of what the goal of the local church is. The typical expectation is of a growing congregation, always faithfully attending, and requiring additions to the building and staff. This growing church adds programs to the ministry and church service, always successful at helping everyone. I've found reality to be more of hitting peaks, then suffering setbacks. I've been left wondering where all the people went. Sometimes I feel like there are more people that used to come to this church than still do. Actually, I know that's true. Ouch! One benefit is that we have a new church every few years!

Another way of thinking about our involvement in people's lives is that of a chain. A chain has many links and each one connects two other links to itself. The chain represents the whole journey of life and each link is a station, or a moment, or a season. The time period that we are involved in people's lives is akin to one of those links. All of the links are necessary to the chain, but none is more important than the others. We need to rejoice that we are one of those links in that person's faith journey. Sadly, one of the links can break, disrupting the journey. When this happens, a delay or a detour occurs in the process of spiritual sanctification.

There are no guarantees in the Live Among Them principle. Our expectation becomes more of doing exactly what Jesus wants us to do and letting the Holy Spirit work in the church member's life. As He does, some are weeded out. They are like that rocky soil that Jesus talks about in Matthew 13. They could not withstand the affliction or persecution that is sure to come. Other attenders find their heart is more like the packed soil along the side of the road. The word is sown, but is quickly snatched up and this member quits coming. Yet others are like the soil with thorns and weeds. They seem to be growing in their walk until the worries of the world or deceitfulness of wealth choke the word out. These go back to the world and may never return.

What did Jesus set as our duty and expectation in Matthew 13? We are to sow in the full knowledge that not every seed will yield a crop. We must be more concerned about how faithfully we carry out our assignment, than the yield.

CONFLICTS AND THREATS

Another expectation that has to be managed is conflict. We wrongly expect that growing a church and growing grace in people's lives will be a smooth journey and if we are truly following Jesus with this "Live Among Them" principle, our life will be peaceful. This is naive. Satan is still out there. As we start pulling people out of his kingdom of darkness, he'll start to defend his territory and his people. You will experience conflicts in both new relationships and long-term relationships in the church. People like status-quo and hate change. Some hate change so much, they will threaten you physically and spiritually. Conflicts and threats will also come from other citizens of the kingdom of darkness. We are taking away one of their own.

I don't ascribe to the axiom of "if we aren't experiencing conflicts and threats we aren't truly making an impact for God." My measure of success isn't based on how successful Satan is in making my life uncomfortable. My measure is how faithfully I am carrying out my assignment for Jesus.

That being said, we are going to have conflicts and threats. They often come from unexpected people or places. Church members often do not like the change in the make-up of the congregation. They will fight you over bringing new people in who don't know how to "church" or to "church" the way they do. New people who aren't churched will ask questions that the so-called mature believers think are stupid. But to the pastor or evangelist they are the questions we want to hear. Questions of discovery. These new attenders will be totally oblivious to church code. They won't know how to dress or what one isn't "allowed to speak of." New kingdom people will make new relationships with people who are different than those of their previous kingdom. Naturally they are going to make mistakes and arguments will arise. People will come to you with complaints or gossip. When this happens, count it all joy. (James 1:1) These are teaching moments! When these pop up figure out how Jesus would deal with the situation and then coach them to do the same.

Remember that our new life in Christ is one of learning. We would not want to leave our old kingdom if the relationships were perfect. The fact of the matter is, we don't know how to have good relationships with others when we aren't in Christ. When we come to Christ our conflicts change and the remedies change. We learn to respond to the threats differently. We used to fight evil with evil but now we're told to overcome evil with good. (Romans 12:21)

NO GOOD DEED GOES UNPUNISHED

Our society has another curious axiom, "no good deed goes unpunished." While this pearl of wisdom might contain some truth, I find the statement very pessimistic. Not my style. My glass is half-full. If you let the pessimistic belief reign you will likely be taken out of the race. You will think, "no matter what I do, no matter how good of a thing I do—I suffer." And you will quit doing good. The Bible tells us to not grow weary in doing good. (Galatians 6:9) The axiom is also arrogant. We are giving ourselves too much credit in thinking we've done something good—that we know what is good and we've certainly performed a good deed. The deed might simply be something we feel should be perceived as good by the receiving person, when in reality the deed is offensive or detrimental to them. This happens because we really haven't taken the time to Live Among Them or walk a mile in their shoes.

SERVE THEM ANYWAY

Earlier I said that conflicts and threats will come as you try to Live Among Them in good faith with good intentions. I said that you will see people depart in anger or faithlessness, yet they still live in your community. You cannot avoid running into each other. You could not get them to see the wrong in their side of the conflict. Maybe you are in the wrong and they leave because of that. Now what do you do? Do you treat them as a tax-collector? Do you endeavor to have nothing to do with them? Do you pretend not to see them when you are both in the grocery store? No, no, and no. You serve them anyway.

You likely served them before they came to church and maybe that is what caused them to come. You still live in the same community together. Remember I pointed out earlier that there are more people who used to come to church than those who still attend church? If we take the tact of "cutting them off" when they leave, you are going to have an awful lot of people you have to pretend you don't see in the grocery store!

Take note that other people will see how you treat this ex-church member. Do you still exhibit the love and grace of Jesus or have you "taken out the trash?" This other person who is watching might be trying to decide whether to come to church or even leave church based on what they see. Oh, the disciple's job is never done! Being cognizant of this is a good challenge for us. Do we truly love like Jesus or not? This does not mean we won't be sad when they leave, even Jesus felt sorrowful when people fell away. Since we have the Holy Spirit in us, we can endure through these changing and often failed relationships. This leads me to my next point... .

STAY BEYOND THE ARGUMENT

We need to stay beyond the argument. What I mean is, never get to the point where we cut people out of our lives. Recognize these fractures for what they are. Come to expect them. We know that in Christ we are immortal and that the kingdom to come means there is no end. Hang in there through the arguments and fractures because many times they mend. Relationships are repaired or worked through. People will return to church. Don't hold on to your side of the issue too tightly. Let the offense slip away. In fact, there is so much joy and beauty when you get to the point where you can look back together over the years of your relationship and remember the tough times. And here you are—still together. Never give up hope that the issue will be forgotten or repaired. We have a *living* hope, amen? We have a love that never gives up. A love described in I Corinthians, "*Love is patient, love is kind and is not jealous; love does not brag and is not arrogant, does not act unbecomingly; it does not seek its own, is not provoked, does not take into account a wrong suffered, does not rejoice in unrighteousness, but rejoices with the truth; bears all things, believes all things, hopes all things, endures all things. Love never fails;*" 1 Corinthians 13:4-8a

SWITCHING HATS

You might be thinking, "easy for you to say" or "I've tried this...doesn't work for me." I've used another handy principle to help me with this challenge. I call the technique, "Switching Hats."

Every walk of life seems to have a dress code. In fact, the way we dress reveals our cultural affinities. If you're a farmer, you dress a certain way. You have a farmer hat and farmer boots. If you're a cowboy, you have a certain hat and boots. If you are a chef, you have an apron and a chef's hat. If you are a fashionista, you dress on the cutting edge of fashion. We visually convey our relationship with others by the way we dress and the hat (literally or figuratively) we are wearing. In ministry we wear a certain type of clothing that represents our ministerial relationship. This is what the clerical collar conveys. Most of us don't literally wear a clerical collar, but to the ones to whom we are ministering, that is what they see. Or maybe they see you wearing a halo because they think you've been an angel to them. Even better, maybe they see you cloaked in a robe of love and peace. Along comes this fracture we've been speaking of. We are stripped of our hats, boots and clerical collars and form of dress in their eyes. Our relationship is now changed. We are no longer in the same role with them. Time for us to switch hats.

This phrase, "switch hats", conveys a change. We now have a different relationship. However, still a relationship. Our part in the relationship has changed. We are no longer fellow church members. They left the family. Or they were sent out of the family. Things are not the same and they won't be. But our assignment from Jesus is to continue to "serve them anyway." So switch hats. Take on a new role in your relation-ship. Maybe a return to the previous relationship. They are now part of the general community and not a fellow church member in spiritual fellowship. This change does not mean to cut them off or hate them, rather to serve them as you would anyone else who isn't part of the church fellowship.

Even though people may have separated from the church, remember, we still Live Among Them. God put us in that community. Our church is within the community. The church is the spiritual center of the community. Non-attenders strangely feel they belong to "their" church, even though they don't attend. Those who are mad at the church or mad at God still acknowledge the church as part of their community—because we are "living among them."

We are in the world, not of the world. This is best illustrated as we Live Among Them.

CHAPTER 8

Needed Spiritual Skills

- Know Life Purpose
- Being Willing
- Identifying to Whom You Best Relate
- Being Shapeable
- He's Already Told You
- Just Being There
- Don't Plan Too Much (leave room for God's Plans)
- Praying Without Ceasing
- Walk the Talk

KNOW LIFE PURPOSE

Do you know your life purpose? Certainly our primary one is to know the only true God, and Jesus Christ whom He has sent. Beyond that, most Christians haven't spent time thinking about this from a servant standpoint. The knowledge of one's life purpose isn't mandatory but can certainly be helpful. I think older people tend to have a better idea of their life purpose because they've tried many things and either succeeded or failed. Younger people are still going through the successes and failures.

If you are the "chief instigator" of the Live Among Them ministry, you might find taking an inventory of your personal skill set and personality helpful. Overlay them onto any community ministry strategy you might have. How do they fit? Are there gaps? If so, consider filling them in with other people having complimentary skills. This is not to say that you shouldn't try new things that you aren't equipped for, but wisdom suggests you consider your skills. Try to discern what your personal life purpose is and whether you have a specific spiritual calling.

To give you an example, my personal mission statement or purpose in life is *"To be a catalyst of grace in others' lives."* I'm expecting that if I live like Jesus by extending grace, love, and mercy to everyone, (especially the lost, abandoned, angry and self-righteous) lives can and will be changed.

What is a spiritual calling? The phrase is one of those churchy expressions we use to communicate the basis for our spiritual vocation. As the term applies to the individual, it is an inner urge, divinely inspired. You'll know if you have a calling when you just can't say no to the calling. There's nothing else you feel you want to do. When you try to do something else, you feel no passion or satisfaction in that endeavor. Knowing your calling can be very comforting, encouraging, and motivating.

BEING WILLING

Hospitality, giving, and helping are spiritual gifts that are extremely helpful when "Living Among Them."

HOSPITALITY: To warmly welcome people, even strangers, into one's home or church as a means of serving those in need of food or lodging. (paraphrased) 1 Peter 4:9,10

GIVING: To share what material resources you have with liberality and cheerfulness without thought of return. (paraphrased) Romans 12:8

HELPING: To render support or assistance to others in the body so as to free them up for ministry. (paraphrased) 1 Corinthians 12:28

Willingness, while not a spiritual gift, is a requirement. The prophet Isaiah was willing. He didn't perceive himself to be qualified, but definitely willing. As with any Bible character, we will have times we don't feel like going on. Willingness might be all we have in those moments. Maybe. We must be willing to go, willing to give, willing to believe, willing to give up things that are important to us, willing to lay up our treasures in heaven. Are you? If not, begin praying for that willing spirit.

IDENTIFYING TO WHOM YOU BEST RELATE

In your personal inventory, attempt to identify the type of people to whom you best relate. People you find easy to communicate with. People who are living in the darkness you once lived in. This might reveal the location or the group of people you start the Live Among Them ministry with.

Or not. For example, Jonah really didn't want to go to the Ninevites. They weren't friends of the Jews. But that is where God wanted him to go. At the end of the day, God knows best. As the chapter on Foreign Mission Trips demonstrated, maybe the best people to go to are those who are entirely different. You may quickly grow to love them.

We've talked in a previous chapter about ministering to people with the ministry you've been given. Specifically, using your experiences in life to empathize with people going through the same things. You may not share all of their life experiences, but God can work through any shortcomings or inexperience we have. If you are searching for a place to start, this principle of identifying similarities might be that place to start your Live Among Them ministry.

BEING SHAPEABLE

Are you shapeable? Maybe another way to ask this is, are you teachable? Our life and character are shaped by a multitude of experiences whereby we arrive at our convictions. Convictions are settled matters. Even with convictions, we need to be shapeable or teachable. We need to be open to challenging our beliefs when we encounter compelling moments. I hope this book is one of those in your life. I pray that you have an open heart to the calling of Jesus and are not so bound into the way things have always been done that you cannot entertain the message of this book. I always like to say to ministry leaders, "Blessed are the flexible."

Being shapeable means we should revisit our convictions with scripture, when they are challenged. We need to determine if they are biblical, tradition or philosophy, or something that is left open to personal conviction. There are things specifically addressed in the Bible, things the Bible is silent about, and general principles that the Bible teaches, which we use to develop a conviction. This is the beauty of older Christians who have a lifetime of experience in testing.

HE'S ALREADY TOLD YOU

Does God want you to do more than be born-again and attend church? Does He want you to have a personal ministry of some form? Should you go on a mission trip? Are you to engage in serving others through some form of compassion ministry?

Christians frequently struggle with knowing God's will on a matter. We are right to ask God before we arrive at a decision. Where Christians err is waiting until they hear an audible command or unmistakable sign confirming the answer. You know...the burning bush thing. This approach of waiting for that audible voice is prone to overlooking what God *has already told us* in the Bible. God has told us to do the majority of ministry mentioned in this book. The how and where are often left up to the minister's choice or creativity as well as what part to play.

I find that reluctance is usually couched in a prejudice or trauma. Other times the hesitation is a matter of taste or simple laziness. And for sure, any ministry effort must be one God calls us to do. I am often asked to do things that are perfectly biblical and good, but not what I believe God wants me to do right then. And I can't do everything. If this is you,

you are off the hook! Enjoy the book. Receive what you can. However, I implore you to at least examine your heart to see what the reason might be for holding off. Just as the local church is a body made up of different parts, the worldwide church is made up of different churches, all forming a kingdom. We each do what God calls us to do.

JUST BEING THERE

Just Being There. Put another way, the ministry of presence. I cannot overstate the value of this and the impact on people's lives. This shouldn't be too hard to understand. In much the same way as the Holy Spirit is always with us, quiet yet always ready to listen and act—our quiet, still presence can be extremely helpful to another.

Just Being There is a prime technique for hospital visits. Sit in the room with the hospitalized, pray silently, only engage in conversation at the level they lead with. Be sensitive to this. Don't feel that you have to entertain them or bring miraculous healing. Pray silently and be attentive to the Holy Spirit. Help with their physical needs as they ask, don't pester them. Reading the Bible to them without preaching can be very soothing. Don't turn the visit into a marathon reading session.

Just Being There for those who have lost a loved one or experienced a violent trauma is a calming and grounding force. They will remember your visit for years. If this situation is connected with someone who died, understand that the one who is grieving will say outlandish things about where their loved one is and what they are doing. Do not debate them.

They probably will not remember what they said anyway. Let the Holy Spirit minister to them.

Just Being There infers listening. Don't hijack the conversation with your experiences or your stories. Listen to theirs and if you must talk, talk about their experiences. Oddly enough, after the shock has passed they will remember you for being such a good counselor!

If you are known as a "talker," this form of ministry might be a real learning curve. I am confident we can do all of these things through Christ who strengthens us, amen?

DON'T PLAN TOO MUCH (LEAVE ROOM FOR GOD'S PLANS)

Don't Plan Too Much. Those who are the planning type, may fall prey to the demon of over-organization (yeah, I don't know if there really is this type of demon.) Why is this a topic of Live Among Them? We need to leave room for God to work in the situations and circumstances. If we've over-planned and are intently focused on accomplishing every nuance of the plan, we are likely to crowd God out. The quiet moments, the times when boredom sets in, can be when God does something special. However, don't take this principle to the other extreme and forgo all planning.

Back in chapter six of this book, I revealed how Living Among Them in Samaria did not qualify as our "Plan A". God did many amazing things through our willingness to be flexible (you know...after we exhausted all of *our* plans). I plead guilty to putting too much of my plan into the process. Nevertheless, I learned many great life lessons out of the whole experience. The point being, even when we don't execute God's plans perfectly, God is perfect and brings about the perfect result. Tuck this nugget away somewhere for recall later when your efforts to carry out Live Among Them go awry.

PRAYING WITHOUT CEASING

This is not a book on prayer, rather a book about ministry that requires a lot of prayer. No question, we need to be people of prayer. I'll leave the "how" up to you and God. My point is that we need to be talking and listening to God all day long as we attempt these mighty things in the name of Jesus.

This might be obvious to the reader, but if we are praying without ceasing, most likely our eyes are open, our hands are not folded, nor are we on our knees. We might even be driving. Is this allowed? Of course! We are carrying on in a attitude of prayer while we execute being the hands of feet of Jesus. We also pray with the people we are helping—right then, out loud as needed. If we are stuck in the middle of our plan, we pray and ask God to open a door or redirect us. We might ask if we heard Him correctly earlier. Has the plan changed? Is He causing a divine delay for my blessing? He is a mighty God. His providence knows no end.

WALK THE TALK

Walk the Talk. The world is watching what we do. Are we kind? Is our speech proper and charitable? Do we listen? How do we handle setbacks and disappointments? How do we treat others? How do we manage our anger? Do we do the things we preach?

A common trap for Christians is trying to be perfect or live up to some preconceived notion of what a Christian is. The world isn't judging us on whether we have a problem-free life, people judge us on how we go through life. They are looking to see who or what we rely on. This is where the expression of "Walk the Talk" emanates. Success at this isn't a singular event. The attribute is measured over time as the variety of life issues occur. I believe that unless we have scars and bruises from life's trials and tribulations, we haven't truly walked the talk. The Christian walk is spiritually opposed to that of the world. The Spirit in us will provoke a spiritual response from the devil. God has said in the book of James that He too is using trials and tribulations to give our faith endurance. My wife and I have a standing joke that unless I'm bleeding I haven't really done any work. Maybe this fits you too?

Count it all joy!

CHAPTER 9

But Wait!

- I Already Have a House
- Our Church Already Has a Building
- Our Church Isn't Flourishing or Prepared
- This Sounds too Messy
- Those People!

"But Wait! I have questions. I have objections. You haven't heard them. Your teaching just isn't practical or evidence-based. You just don't understand our area. This is way too risky; I can't put my people at risk like this. I don't have the time necessary. Our people simply aren't going to be interested in doing this."

I ALREADY HAVE A HOUSE

"I already have a house. I've been here a long time and don't feel like moving. I'm not sure I could afford to move."

I hear you. My wife and I bought a house in Samaria even though we could find better areas for investment and quality of living. But this is where God wanted us. For His purpose. Pray about God's purpose for your life. Pray whether you should consider moving. You might even need to drive over to "that" neighborhood and see how He answers. Don't get me wrong. I'm not saying you have to move, but you might be missing out on many blessings by not doing so. Living in the midst of the people you are serving, saves a lot of driving time. You can be more efficient. You will have opportunities that you wouldn't otherwise.

OUR CHURCH ALREADY HAS A BUILDING

Our church already has a building. I might not be as charitable on this answer as the previous one. What is your church's purpose? Most churches have a catchy mission statement that is rather canned. Their building is nice. Some are *very* nice. The grounds are finished, including playgrounds. The inside is finished, neat, and tidy. The church has been there a long time. Or just a short time. "*..If we move, many of our well-to-do people are not going to follow us. They don't want to drive into that neighborhood or sit next to 'those people...'*"

This decision requires much prayer and solid leadership. The answer might not be an "either/or" but a "both/and." You won't know until you pray. Most churches are too comfortable, so this challenge might pinch a little. This comfort has possibly caused a loss of purpose or passion. To these objections I ask, "Can't God do a great work again? And when did you feel most spiritually alive—when you were comfortable or when you were struggling?" I know my answer.

You might consider sending some spies out into the land. Let them get their feet wet. Let them get a feel for the people and situations. Then let them report back to the church. I don't mean a one-hour drive around either. Get out. Knock on doors. Ask questions. Do things. Look for residents who want to help you. Look for opportunities, not how large the giants of the land are. Start a house church or Bible study there. Then start a food pantry.

Your church purpose isn't to become wealthy or comfortable. Church life isn't purposed in developing programs and only do those until Jesus returns. The spiritual calling isn't to fellowship with only the people who are coming and already saved. Look again at your church purpose and see if you agree with me.

Many churches have their building paid off and/or a large savings account. Being debt-free is proper, but a savings account? When Jesus returns, we won't need that money. When He returns, we won't need that building. Our children and grandchildren aren't going to be saved because they come to the same church that has been there for four generations. Most children and grandchildren leave town soon as they can. Your building might be an opportunity for another church or a need in the community. How many salvations are you having now? How many weddings? How many water baptisms? I guarantee you, you'll have more of each of these once you move. You might be feeling too weak to start over. I can totally relate to that. But as we examined in a previous chapter, when we are weak then God is strong. When we become weak to reach the weak, God shows up. Ready to slap me yet? Don't, I love you.

Please understand, I don't think my place is to tell you what to do with your church. I'm simply putting forth a topic for you to consider and pray about.

OUR CHURCH ISN'T FLOURISHING OR PREPARED

You may be thinking, "Our church isn't flourishing or prepared to do anything like that." Well, that might be because you haven't tried. Again, consider the ideas given earlier to the church that is comfortable and successful. The same strategies could be employed. Take a hard look at your church—both the building and the people. Critically reflect on the culture of the church, the activities, the relationships, the passion of the worship service, and your mission statement.

Are you and the members having fun "doing" your church? If not, maybe the solution is to bring new life into the church. How? Children. I've found that so many churches lack children. More children is the one thing most members wish they had. However, church members often aren't willing to be flexible with the children or do things with and for the children. Children are messy. Oh, and noisy. You know that. Greater numbers of children are typically found in the working class or poverty areas less so in the high society neighborhoods. I suspect most of us think a flourishing church has many children.

THIS SOUNDS TOO MESSY

This ministry idea sounds too messy. Yes, messy is a good observation. Whether too messy is a judgment call for you to make. Proverbs 14:4 might provide some insight, *"Where no oxen are, the manger is clean, But much revenue comes by the strength of the ox."* Oxen are used for farm work. Since a lot of their work is in the field or mud, the animals can get pretty dirty. They bring that back into the barn with them. If they are working steadily, the farmer will earn much income. If the farmer's barn is clean, the oxen haven't been out working or they simply aren't in the barn. Children are the same way. If they are in the church playing or making crafts or participating in lessons, the church will get messy. The floor will be cluttered, the chairs will be left haphazard and often dirty with craft material or mud. The bathrooms will be messy as they wash up after events. They will track dirt in on their shoes from outside. The lost and found will be full. They don't sit still or quietly. But, like the oxen, if the church is clean there are likely no children. If there are no children, there will likely be fewer people and subsequently less tithing, as well as much less energy.

In much the same way, if there are no unchurched or poor people in the church the premises are very likely clean and tidy. Unchurched people and the poor don't usually have "Sunday-go-to-meeting" shoes or clothing. Their houses are more likely to be surrounded by dirt than manicured lawns. They will typically spend more time outdoors. They are "hands-on" people. All of this adds up to dirt brought in and clothing articles left behind. This group of people doesn't often put dishes away or offer to vacuum up afterwards. Their lives simply aren't very disciplined. But if you need some wood split or your SUV worked on—they are there for you. If you are stuck in a ditch, they have the truck and tow strap to pull you out.

Does this make the Live Among Them ministry idea sound too messy? Again, you decide. I say, "No it doesn't." Their souls are more important to me and Jesus than their discipline or tidiness. I prefer tidiness and cleanliness, but not at the expense of becoming a barrier to people who don't. I think the answer is one of priorities. If you revisit your church mission statement—what does the phrase say? Let's look at eleven typical church mission statements—one might even be your church's. One is a red-herring.

1. To experience the love of Jesus and give it away.
2. Helping people take their next step toward Christ together.
3. People leading People into a life-changing, ever-growing relationship with Jesus Christ.
4. To lead people to become fully devoted followers of Christ.
5. We exist to lead people into a growing relationship with Jesus.
6. To Know Jesus and Make Him Known.
7. God's Family pursuing God's Kingdom.
8. Reach Up, Reach Out, Reach In.
9. To make the name of Jesus famous in our generation.
10. To Revive believers, Reach friends, and Renew Culture.

11. To be available to the righteous and clean for Jesus in His Temple.

Do any of these statements speak about their building? Do any of them speak about teaching them to be tidy and clean before entering? Do any of these statements refer to age or income? Do you recognize the phony one? They *all* speak about people and relationships, except the red-herring I threw in. If we are limiting these statements, are we truly following Jesus? They *all* require action. Obedience to the mission statement means we have to go and do and connect with people. If we're honest, our church behavior might fit the last statement, the red-herring.

THOSE PEOPLE!

Let's deal with the phrases "those people" or "you people" for a moment. We all have uttered both. Usually in disgust. What are we communicating? We're saying they are not part of us and generally not as good as us. Isn't this antithetical to church mission statements and the great commission Jesus gave us? We should not dare think Jesus loves us more than them or that we are better than others. We're all on a journey of faith and at differing waypoints. Some have yet to even reach the beginning with Jesus, but they are on their journey. Let's find a way to intersect with "those people" and introduce them to the love of Jesus. This won't be a single conversation. More likely, an evangelistic effort will require multiple conversations combined with acts of kindness. Hopefully, you will be reading the words of Jesus to them and letting the Holy Spirit convict. On a typical day, people hear the words of the world and seldom the words of Jesus. Let us revise the phrases, "those people" and "you people", to "we" or "us" or "part of us" in an effort to be welcoming.

Yes, I'm totally aware of their lifestyle of sin. And that lifestyle isn't acceptable to Jesus. But creating distance and barriers is generally counterproductive. There are some life-styles that I struggle with too; so this is as much a statement for me as one for you. Jesus wants us to bring them in and let Him convict and clean. This book is totally focused on this dictate.

We can only do these things with the strength that God provides.

CHAPTER 10

Ready, Set, Go!

- Find a Community
- Discover Their Needs
- Provide for Their Needs
- Don't Demand Fruit
- Be Spiritually Ready When They Come
- Develop House Churches

FIND A COMMUNITY

Find a community you feel called to serve. Find a location to make home base within that community. The community should be defined by some geographical boundary. This could be a subdivision or an area of town with its own name. People congregate with people like them—"Birds of a feather flock together." There is at least one common thread. Examples are race, nationality, income, lifestyle, religion, or age. Communities have identifiable commonality.

Our community is made up primarily of working class and poor people. They don't like rules; therefore they don't want to live with a homeowners' association. They want to be in an area where they can either get away from people or at least not feel crowded. We have a lot of veterans. People own guns and dogs and trucks. Every other property looks like a junkyard. We have to haul water from a station to our houses. You can identify someone from this area by the water tank in the back of their truck.

Do you live in this community already? If so, you've got the first step done. If not, begin your search. Drive and pray. Observe the people. See if the area fits the community description above. See if your heart aches for them. Can you relate to them either through current lifestyle or perceived background and culture? I love the mountains, small towns and rural areas, casual dress, unpretentiousness, custom homes, acreage. Oh, and did I mention camping and the outdoors? Sure I did. I've always wanted to live in a campground. I have an affinity with this type of community. These are my people.

Spend time getting to know social services workers. Let them know you are available to help. Meet probation officers and deputies. Go to other churches or food pantries and give them your contact information. Go to rehab centers, homeless shelters, and soup kitchens. Start those free lunches or kids play days. Knock on doors and offer to help.

FIND OUT THEIR NEEDS

Once you are located, figure out what physical needs there

are. Then ask God how you can provide for them. After we situated the church in the house we bought, we determined that a food pantry would be of benefit to the community. Even though there were numerous food pantries in town, they were far away from our community. Many of our residents don't have running vehicles, or driver's licenses, or insurance, registered vehicles, or money for gas. Come to find out, many don't even have a kitchen or bathroom. They live in campers or makeshift sheds. Even tents! Most of the houses are in poor repair and many are surrounded by junk. We don't have public utilities except electricity, and not to the whole area. So we identified their needs as food, transportation, employment, firewood, better housing.

PROVIDE FOR THEIR NEEDS

Then we began to ask God how we could provide for these needs and where to begin. We started with a food pantry. We emptied our cabinets and put the food downstairs in the converted garage that had a separate entrance. I asked around at the local grocery stores, food pantries and restaurants for donations. The common answer given, "Sorry, we already give to so and so and that's all we have." I went to another town about 50 miles away and found a soup kitchen willing and able to share. I drove there once a week to collect food. As time went on, we were able to develop local sources and now we have a hard time giving all of the food away. We serve, on average, 300 people per month in a community of approximately 2000-2500.

Next, we held free lunches in the park. We took grills, tables and utensils to the park every Saturday morning in summer. To promote the event, we set up our homemade signs on Fridays. We posted on the local social media groups. Every week we planned a meal and bought the food. Sometimes local restaurants would donate or sponsor the meal. People loved coming. The event was work, but we had so much fun. The outreach proved very effective in building community and relationships.

Firewood is an issue for people every year here. Wood can be expensive and for most people going into the forest to get their own isn't possible. Our first year, we took a few flatbed trailers to the local lumber mill and received donated logs. Big logs, 10 to 20 inches in diameter. We took them back to the church property and cut them into rounds with chainsaws. We split the rounds and stacked them into a pile. This process drew volunteers. Relationships were built with the volunteers, those in need and the church. The needy came to get wood or requested a delivery. As time went on, homeowners thinning out their property offered their felled trees as a donation. We picked up trees or rounds and brought them to the church to split and stack. We built relationships with these homeowners and tree mitigation companies, too. Each year we had more and more wood to give away. As time went on, the local probation department connected our church with those ordered to do community service. The probationer earned 12 hours if they cut-split-delivered-stacked a cord of wood. Most had 24-28 hours to do and this equated to 2-4 cords of wood. We've grown to gathering 35+ cords of wood using this combination of acquisition and labor. Our only expense now is fuel, after purchasing the chainsaws and splitters. Even some of those were donated.

Another thing we've done for our neighbors is give them rides into town or to work. This is pretty easy for us since there is only one road into town. We don't have mass transit here in Samaria. Residents get out to the highway and catch a ride with a neighbor or someone from church, because they too live in the same community. We help or encourage them to get their driver's license and insurance. If they do, we are often able to help them get a starter car. They are now climbing the economic ladder. Occasionally a car gets donated to us, or we're able to raise funds to buy an inexpensive car. We encourage them to chip in. We dangle this carrot of a car while we watch to see that they are doing things to help themselves. You can't do this if you don't "Live Among Them."

We have a ministry called Helping Hands. Church members and neighbors help with home repairs or clearing out junk from someone's property. Low income residents can't afford weekly trash service. Many have poor credit and can't qualify for the service. Their lives aren't orderly and they don't think ahead to arrange pickup. Therefore, they have trash stacking up they say they're going to take to the dump. But the dump is a long way away. And they might not have a truck or gas or a license. Doesn't take too long to pile up. Moreover, if you are poor, you struggle to say no to people who want to give you things. Even things you don't really need. They pile up. If you don't have a working washer and dryer or the ability to get several miles into town to the laundromat, the easier solution is to accept clothing donations rather than to wash clothes.

These stack up too. If one is given a cheap car that breaks down and they haven't saved up money to pay for repairs, the vehicle just sits. At some point the car can't be started or isn't deemed worth keeping. Rinse and repeat. Now you have multiple vehicles on the property. Tires go flat. Neighbors get irritated. No junkyard is complete without a broken refrigerator or washer and dryer. We offer to help them take things to the dump or recycler. Our church bought a flat bed trailer for this purpose. We loan the trailer out or we help with the task. The trailer is a ministry tool, not an asset.

Another Helping Hands ministry is home repairs. The elderly or wage workers often do not have the time, energy, or money to make repairs. Steps, decks, roofs, fences, plumbing, and electrical, need mending or replacement. One of our members or the pastor will go see what the situation requires and make a plan to help. He or she will gather up a handful of volunteers and dedicate a day or two for the effort. The messy person's neighbors notice what's going on and we build good-will in the community.

Child Protection Services can come into a home and remove the children because conditions aren't safe or clean enough. A church crew can go in and help a parent clean and paint and put child locks on the cabinets, in the hopes of reunifying the family. Maybe the parent needs work, or rides to work, or a trash service, or childcare. Some of these are areas where the church can help short-term and be the bridge to successful living. Occasionally, parents need help holding a garage sale or renting a storage unit and moving their stuff. This is a way for the church to shine.

DON'T DEMAND FRUIT

In all of these efforts and building of relationships, you cannot demand fruit. We have to serve others for Jesus and pray the Holy Spirit convicts hearts. We are responsible for our efforts and not the work of the Holy Spirit. Don't demand they come to church. Invite them, let them decide. Don't demand they listen to a sermon before you give them free food or a free lunch. That approach doesn't work. People can look like they're listening when they've tuned you out. People say they will come to church or read the Bible, but they don't. Endeavor to be witnesses of Jesus, not used car salesmen.

BE SPIRITUALLY READY WHEN THEY COME

Be Spiritually Ready When They Come. Prepare everyone to accept an unchurched, low income, socially offensive visitor. Treat them with respect. Do not lay church rules or biblical commands on them. Be friendly. Talk to them. Don't talk too much. Ask questions about themselves and listen. Don't interrupt with stories about yourself. If you notice they aren't very comfortable or forthcoming, find something in common or humorous. Don't get political. (Whew, I should probably repeat that a dozen times.) Don't gossip about others. Don't brag. Don't criticize. I realize I've just eliminated many typical conversations with newcomers. Seriously, you and your church members might have to practice or role play this.

Learn to converse normally. Don't use "Christianese", or get all mystical. That doesn't build relationships. This may take some practice or at least some attention to what you are saying.

An effective way to become spiritually ready is to go visit a church or two that you've never been to where nobody knows you. This is very easy to do while you are on vacation. Or, just drive to the next town and pick a church. Pay attention to how you feel as a visitor. Does anyone make you comfortable or uncomfortable? How does the church culture and layout make you feel?

Being spiritually ready means getting a good handle on what Jesus says and how to treat the not-yet believer or unchurched. Spend time reading the Bible with this focus.

DEVELOP HOUSE CHURCHES

Develop House Churches. The model used by Church Project really stands out. House churches meet during the week and then all gather at a central place on Sunday. Each house church has a house pastor. The house pastors work with the central church pastor and elders. A house church consists of a maximum of 10-12 people. They discuss the teaching from Sunday and take their study and understanding a little deeper through questions and conversation. House church differs from a small group Bible study. Small groups typically have their own track, no house pastor, and are affinity based rather than geographically based. A house church functions like a miniature version of the central church.

In a previous chapter, I challenged you to sell your house or church and move *into* the neighborhood. That may not be practical, or possible, or maybe you just aren't ready for that step yet. Planting house churches that are connected to your church might be an excellent way to get your feet wet and really learn the where, why, how, who of the whole Live Among Them adventure. This strategy can mix the best of both worlds.

The house pastor functions much the same as a local church pastor does. He is the first point of contact for the members. He is responsible for teaching, discipling, charitable needs, pastoral care and so on. Each member is tasked with inviting people to their house church. Once the group outgrows the 10-12 size, a new group or house church is formed. The house church is not autonomous. The small body is linked to and a part of the central church. The central church leads in the spiritual direction and messages for the body and performs the oversight and administrative functions.

This method of house church meets the Live Among Them challenge.

CHAPTER 11

Grace Givers

- Grace Is
- Giving Grace
- Grace Growers
- Grace in Action
- We Need Scars
- A Life of Grace Realized

GRACE IS

This is Grace: *Now we who are strong ought to bear the weaknesses of those without strength and not just please ourselves. Each of us is to please his neighbor for his good, to his edification. For even Christ did not please Himself; but as it is written, "THE REPROACHES OF THOSE WHO RE-PROACHED YOU FELL ON ME." For whatever was written in earlier times was written for our instruction, so that through perseverance and the encouragement of the Scriptures we might have hope. Now may the God who gives perseverance and encouragement grant you to be of the same mind with one another according to Christ Jesus, so that with one accord you may with one voice glorify the God and Father of our Lord Jesus Christ.*

Therefore, accept one another, just as Christ also accepted us to the glory of God. For I say that Christ has become a servant to the circumcision on behalf of the truth of God to confirm the promises given to the fathers, and for the Gentiles to glorify God for His mercy. Romans 15:1-9a.

And Jesus is grace. *"For the Law was given through Moses; grace and truth were realized through Jesus Christ."* John 1:17

Grace is God's empowering presence enabling us to do what He has called us to do. Grace is God's power realized in Jesus, in abundance. Grace is the method of divinely dealing in salvation and in the believer's life and service. *Giving* Grace is a spiritual act containing the characteristics of God's grace, extended to someone.

"As each one has received a special gift, employ it in serving one another as good stewards of the manifold grace of God." 1 Peter 4:10   We have received the gift of grace. We are tasked to reproduce grace and to give it away in serving one-another. Grace residing in us is critical, if we are going to Live Among Them.

Grace is freely given. It empowers people for service. Grace is promised to the humble, because God is opposed to the proud. Grace is benevolence and favor.

GIVING GRACE

Giving Grace: A spiritually apprised act containing the characteristics of God's grace extended to someone. Grace is fueled by mercy, love, peace. Recognize grace moments. Revel in them.

What is a grace moment? A slice of time when grace is extended to someone and is abundantly evident. Grace moments strung together create a *life of grace*. A grace moment can occur as you are talking to someone and encouraging them or when you stop and give help to the needy. A grace moment blossoms as you take mail wrongly delivered to your address over to your neighbor. Grace is given when you forgive someone or teach them to forgive their trespasser. Grace absolutely exists when a trespasser is forgiven. So a grace moment is when God's grace is passed through you to another and is palpably experienced.

What did I mean earlier when I encouraged *you* to be a grace catalyst? Examples were just given. Going forward, be the spark that starts the flame of grace.

GRACE GROWERS

Grace Growers. Believers are to be *grace givers*. There are people in our lives who are the *grace growers*. They are those who need grace from us.

How do we grow in grace? Let love and humility be your guides. Surprise the needy one with grace, aim for the conscience, and allow the grace grower to feel the consequences of his actions. Just like Jesus, if you love someone for the glory of God, you will be less controlled by the grace grower and their erratic or ungodly behavior.

Do most of your analysis on your own heart, not your grace-grower's heart. Remember that you have been given mercy (what you don't deserve). You will be able to help the other person see his sins in ways that are not hypocritical. If your self-examination is biblically guided, God will help you to see clearly. You won't feel as crazy or filled with self-doubt. You will remember how you were once a grace-grower for someone else!! We need to accept grace-growers into the church, and corporately, we need to love them. Do not fight your individual grace-growers. Value them.

Grace growers truly are a blessing in our lives. Initially, we feel they are the irritants. And that is *exactly* what they are. The irritation is like that piece of sand in the oyster that causes a pearl to grow. The pearl of grace should grow in us as a result of that. Give thanks to God for the *grace growers* He puts in our lives! These difficult people and circumstances are often the tools God uses to bring forth the enduring beauty of Christian character.

Now go and find a *grace grower* to love on.

GRACE IN ACTION

This is what grace in action looks like: *We urge you, brethren, admonish the unruly, encourage the fainthearted, help the weak, be patient with everyone. See that no one repays another with evil for evil, but always seek after that which is good for one another and for all people.* 1 Thessalonians 5:14-22

True grace will have the characteristics of God's grace:

- Peaceful, peacemaking
- Sound Judgment, Sober
- Patient, Sees the bigger picture
- Loving, Love for One Another
- Holy, Righteous, Just
- Pure, not deceptive
- Good-willed
- Humble (Amazing Grace Hymn)
- Truthful
- Not Condemning
- Edifying, Encouraging
- Empathetic, Sympathetic

WE NEED SCARS

Without scars we cannot know grace intimately. We won't be able to extend grace to others. Jesus had scars. Do you have any? The scars are realized through shared experiences—not "kum-by-yah" moments. Suffering afflictions, then receiving comfort and grace, plows up the soil of our hearts. This process is a necessary prerequisite for us to employ grace in serving others.

A LIFE OF GRACE REALIZED

God ceaselessly works through grace, to impart to us and perfect in Him, corresponding grace. Reproduce. Give it away. Grace is the connecting goo of spiritual relationships. Jesus extended love, grace, mercy to us. To the outcast, to the downtrodden, to the chief of all sinners. And we too should do this. We were once lost ourselves. I used to be that *grace grower*.

A life of grace can be realized through a Live Among Them ministry. You will be either blessed with grace giving opportunities or challenged to give grace when you truly don't want to. A Live Among Them ministry cannot be conducted without grace.

Grace and peace to you.

CHAPTER 12

The Toolbox

- Benevolence
- Become a Community Service Location
- Open a Food Pantry
- Begin a Firewood Ministry
- Marry, Bury, Visit
- Identification Paperwork Services
- Repair Things
- Discipleship through Work
- Take Out the Garbage
- Emergency Shelter

This Toolbox is the day-to-day manual for carrying out a Live Among Them ministry. This box is a compilation of methods and processes gained over ten years of intensive field work.=

BENEVOLENCE

Our church has two benevolence tracks, 1) members, 2) community. We handle each one with specific guidelines. The Bible gives us direction on each. I've included a sample policy and process that you are free to use or modify. We keep separate ledgers on each. Any funds that the church members donate to the church benevolence are kept apart and used specifically for those needs. The general benevolence expenses are tracked as Community Reach efforts.

The *member benevolence* is our modern-day way of living out Acts 2. Members bring cash into the church for the elders or deacons to distribute in the manner we read in the books of Acts, Timothy, Peter, and James. This fund is used for member emergencies rather than "too much month left at the end of their paycheck." Our church also budgets or allocates a portion of the treasury to be used for *community benevolence*. Examples of these needs are: gas for their car, money to buy automotive repair parts, propane to heat their camper, or personal toiletries. These are usually smaller ticket items. I typically have beneficiaries donate a little of their time doing some chores around the church. Not every situation fits this mold and often we'll just help out with the $25-50 need. I sometimes put gas in their car or propane tank myself. We rarely buy cigarettes and never marijuana or alcohol (and yes, people ask for these). We often help with prescriptions. When people ask for a loan, we say, "No, we are a church, not a bank. If we can't give you the financial help, we aren't going to give you a loan either." Giving someone in need a loan generally creates new problems. They now have a debt, no way to make payments, and are put in a position of making excuses. This is not the way to build relationships for Jesus. Give charity, don't loan charity.

A word of caution: When conducting the Benevolence Interview included in the Appendix, don't act like a Bank Loan Officer sitting at a desk, taking an application. Keep the general questions in mind and just carry on a normal conversation weaving in those questions. In short, try to find out what they've done to help themselves. Often I find that the conversation reveals an issue that forestalls the cash benevolence. Help them find their own solution. This is the best outcome. Many times the solution doesn't pop up quickly, but requires more questions and discussion. Become a sounding board for them and often the two of you will come up with a solution or an action step.

A second word of caution: When completing the Benevolence Application included in the Appendix, be sensitive to how thorough you need to be on the line items. Church members often feel guilty about how they spend their money and can feel judged by you asking the question.

How do you say "no" while still being helpful? "I can't do that for you today, but I can do _____ for you." When you interview them, listen for clues and ideas on what to fill the blank with. This technique works miracles.

Don't overlook the ministry opportunity of praying for this person—regardless of whether or not the church agrees to give money. This is how you teach that God is working in their life.

BECOME A COMMUNITY SERVICE LOCATION

Being a Community Service Location is a unique way of meeting those who are wrestling with their life choices. The church that chooses to engage in this and is trying to meet needs in the community, will find this unique ministry to be a win-win. Here is how the process works: County corrections and probation offices are charged with supervising court-ordered community service for those who have been charged with crimes. The crimes range from not showing up for court, a probation violation, drunk driving, drug violations, domestic violence, theft, trespassing, driving without a license, and so on. Some crimes will be of a more heinous and violent nature, such as murder or sexual offenses. The more serious offenses require incarceration long before someone is released with probation requirements. They will not be fresh off the crime, when they show up for service days. Many categories of convictions require weekly testing for drugs and alcohol. Our church serves as a meeting place for mobile alcohol and drug testers of those who cannot make it into town.

Typically, people are ordered to perform a specified number of hours of community service work. They have to pay to enroll in the program and must do the service at approved locations. They can't say, "I helped my neighbor take out their trash and I carried an old lady's groceries to her car. Give me 1 hour of credit." Your church will communicate to the probation officers what tasks you'll have the volunteers do. The probation officers will inform their probationers of the possible locations and type of tasks they can do to fulfil their service. Churches with thrift stores will often have hours available for receiving donations, sorting and shelving. Every church can use extra janitorial help or maintenance. Our church has a firewood ministry to provide free wood to the needy during the winter. The probationer earns 12 hours for every cord they cut-split-deliver-stack.

Why would a church consider having convicts work on their building or property, often inside? (grin) The situation allows the minister to have practical spiritual discussions that flow naturally. They can't run away from you, because they've agreed to do the service. Personally, I don't bring up how stupid they were, they usually do that on their own. I bring up the positive side of how they are helping others. For many, this is the first time they've helped others while getting nothing in return. Most crimes have a root of selfishness. They steal because they have desires but they don't want to work to earn the money. They drive without a license because they refuse to pay their traffic fines or child-support. They don't appear at court when ordered, because they don't feel like showing up. I like to make them feel the good in helping others. Some might actually come to church and join the family. At the very least, I am kind to them. I usually work along with them. This becomes true one-on-one discipleship.

OPEN A FOOD PANTRY

A Food Pantry is almost a given practice of Living Among Them and the old way to do Church. First create or designate an area to be the Food Pantry. You'll need shelving, a table, a refrigerator, a freezer. Someone will have to serve as the "director". Identify specific days and hours you will distribute.

A "hunter and gatherer" is needed to look for donations and pick them up. Operationally, you need to collect statistics. A form with name, number of people in the household, age brackets of household, and a signature is all that's needed. Total out each of these statistics every month. Some donors will want a report submitted with these totals.

A word of caution: Do *not* go overboard and require identification, evidence of need, financial documents, etc. You are not a Food Bank. Your objective should be to give out food to all that ask. Don't prejudge or require them to tell you their story. Asking for food is humiliating enough. Your objective is to give all of the food away—not be a bank, storing food. God will fill vacuums, not full storehouses. Trust Him. Watch and see!

Your local health department might have rules you have to follow. Typically, the rules are more extensive if you serve prepared food. There are rules for repackaging bulk food into portions. There are refrigeration and freezing rules. Most of them are basic to the food service worker. A good idea, which might also be required by the local health department, is to have at least one of the workers Safe Serve™ certified. This is a certification most restaurant workers possess. Obtaining the certification is pretty simple and can often be done online. The director might need a manager level certification. You might have people who are already certified offering to work the food pantry. God is good this way.

When you first start out, you'll likely find collecting do-nated food to be difficult.. Trust me when I say food sourcing will get easier. Start with your own cabinets. Maybe have a food drive within your church as a seed to start. Use some of the church treasury to buy food. Another word of caution: Don't buy the cheapest junk food! Pretend you are buying for your own family. Don't overload on processed or canned foods either. We aren't trying to kill them off early! Most grocery stores have a donation process of near-expired foods. States have a grant program of funding through the Department of Social Services. Feeding America is a national food bank that distributes regionally to food banks such as Care and Share. You can enroll in their network by meeting some basic requirements. Usually they offer food at very low prices and small delivery charges. At first, the solution will seem like going to Walmart would be easier. Over the long haul you'll find the unadvertised specials that come through the food pantry networks. Enrolling in a food pantry network is definitely worth the time and spending of church treasury funds. Even health food grocery stores have donation programs for food pantries. The bottom line, there is not just one source for food. Be open to ideas and search for any avenue possible. Community members will donate food cards or cash to your food bank once they hear of you. Vacationers or those moving out of town will donate food as they empty their pantries.

BEGIN A FIREWOOD MINISTRY

A Firewood Ministry works much the same as a Food Pantry. This ministry is one that men are particularly drawn to and gives them a way to shine. During the summer and early fall, collect wood and stack somewhere on your church property. Leak out the word that wood is available to the needy. People tend to self-regulate whether they are "the needy" so don't confront them with paperwork requirements. This ministry draws in donors, volunteers, and the needy to your church. What a great thing! Chapter ten has more detail on this ministry.

MARRY, BURY, VISIT

Marry, Bury, Visit. These are basic functions of the church. But often we only offer them to church members. If you've read to this point and consider your whole community as part of your church, you'll see the opportunity presented by the requests. Standard church operating procedure is to offer these services only to current members, to those who have been through a class, or a member who has taken ill, been hospitalized or moved to a nursing home. The reasoning behind offering these services exclusively to current church members is typically based on the faulty premise they are deemed more worthy and holy; or too often, improper manipulation to coerce non-members into membership. Sometimes it is a way to justify declining the request because the non-member doesn't meet the "club standard". They are too rough, unrefined, don't drive a nice car, or not holy enough to enhance the church image. Maybe they have been to jail, have tattoos, or facial piercings. These are people that Jesus loves and they need ministry just like any other demographic.

I have openly advertised and promoted to people who are living together, that we would give them a free wedding. You heard me right. Again, standard church operating procedure is to insist they separate, move out, and stay celibate for six months while they go through your class. I've tried this and nobody has done this. If we believe God wants men and women to be married and not "live in sin", let's be part of the solution. I've met so many people who wanted to get married but could not find a church or pastor to marry them. Why? The objections include, "they are already living together, they are divorced, or they aren't a member of our church." The list goes on. The process of organizing a wedding gives you a counseling or discipleship moment and possibly a new family to welcome into your church. At the very least, they aren't "living in sin" anymore.

Be willing to conduct funerals or memorial services for those in the community who aren't members of your church. Why should we refuse because the deceased lived as a heathen? They are no longer here. We cannot change that. The service is for the living who assemble. The gathering is an opportunity to weave in the gospel—given our common fate of death. You don't have to declare that the pagan went to heaven nor do you have to tell everyone the person went to hell. But you can talk about each place and what the Bible says about them. You can remind all that we each have this day coming and we might give some thought to our plight. Your church will be remembered by family and community members and your service will come up in conversation along with memories of the deceased. You will be viewed as part of the community and as their church.

Visit people. Visit those who live in your community, or are in the hospital, jail, and nursing homes. Be known as one who does that. Give people rides to and from these places. Give them rides to the pharmacy or grocery store. Give them rides to their probation or court appointments. Sit with them in court. You are going through life with them. Why? Because you *Live Among Them.* Don't be afraid, you won't get stained. You will get blessed. Guaranteed.

IDENTIFICATION PAPERWORK SERVICES

Help with identification paperwork. Low income people, elderly, medically afflicted, recently released convicts, and the homeless, all suffer from the loss of identification. In fact, you'll find that a lot of people who are unemployed don't have identification. Identification is needed for everything—except voting. Sorry for that. But truly, if they want food stamps, they have to have I.D. They need various forms of identification to find a job, get their driver's license back, buy insurance, and register a vehicle. Most people needing I.D. don't have internet access, often not even a cell phone, aren't good with paperwork, and frequently can't read well. They don't have the money for replacement documents or renewal fees and fines. You may be in shock as you are confronted with this situation.

Close your mouth, put your eyeballs back in their sockets, and put on your best grace face. Take inventory of what they have by way of identification and what they've tried already. The basics are, birth certificate, Social Security card, State I.D. or driver's license. At least two of these are required for employment. This is why so many people work "under the table." They don't have these documents and employers may look the other way in exchange for paying wages with cash and not the withholdings required by the government. This is illegal and we want to encourage people to live lawfully.

The process for establishing identification may include looking up the hospital in the county in which they were born and requesting a duplicate birth certificate. You'll pay a fee of $10-25. Visiting or calling the local Social Security office will gain a duplicate Social Security card. Obtaining a state I.D. card or driver's license is usually the most difficult and expensive. The state office will require a bevy of documents for either. Examples are: two or three evidences of county residence such as a rental agreement, bills mailed to a permanent address, or a property deed. More pieces of I.D. are also needed, such as a birth certificate, social security card, or student photo I.D., or library card, and paystubs. This effort can get pretty frustrating when you can't get one I.D. because you don't have the other I.D. You will quickly gain empathy for the frustration experienced by the person you are helping. Help with the fees as you see fit. Give them the money, don't make a loan. Remember, you aren't a bank, so don't be a lender. Don't put them in the spot of failing to honor a vow. This help is intentioned in giving them a hand up.

REPAIR THINGS

People need help with auto or home repairs. The cost for professional help is way beyond their ability. So they just let the needed repairs go until the undone turns into a catastrophe. Their car becomes one of those sitting in the yard for years on end and their house becomes a decrepit fixer-upper, eye sore. Help them for free. Even buy the parts.

The process that works best is for the pastor (or whomever receives the call) to meet with the person to assess the problem. The problem, not the person! This is a critical step. When you gather volunteers or experts, you need to know what parts might be needed, the cost, and what expertise or labor is required. Often, this site visit exposes something different than the phone call revealed. Sometimes the extent of the damage requires you to put a limit on what you can offer, or explain what you can't offer. This assessment meeting is an absolutely divine opportunity. You were *invited* to their house for a face-to-face discussion. Yet another word of caution: Do not take your Bible in and preach first, or show them their sin and how their carnal behavior is the root of the problem. Don't tell them they deserve the problem and how they should have prevented the problem with better decisions. They already know this. Do be grace-filled, empathetic, with your listening ears on, not your wagging tongue talking about yourself. Did I just violate my own rules about not preaching and instead being grace-filled? I hope not.

Organize a work day, your volunteer team, the tools needed, and buy the parts or materials in advance (to the extent you can). Arrive, greet the person, and love on them for a moment. Organize work tasks and assignments. Be sensitive about letting the homeowner take the lead or helping. Do not spend all day talking to the person if they aren't able to work. However, you might find that one volunteer's task is to hang out with the person. Get to work. Have fun, but do the work. Don't keep patting yourself on the back or digging for compliments from the person you are helping.

When you finish, just tell the person they are welcome. Don't elaborate on why you helped them or what you expect, etc. Ask if you can pray for them or bless their house. Then leave. And rejoice in your car.

DISCIPLESHIP THROUGH WORK

A "top-secret" but time proven technique of discipleship is, Discipleship through Work. Find something you need to have done and hire the homeless or unemployed. Consider working alongside your helper and give them some pocket-money when finished. While you are working together, you will have moments when they bring up a topic or disclose something about their life. In turn, you have the prime opportunity to pour into them. Because you are working at a task, the moments between conversations are not uncomfortable. Each of you can think of responses and what to say next. Remember, communication starts with listening. Being slow to speak. Empathizing. Building relationship. I call this discipleship through work ministry "stealth evangelism". Give them pocket money, even though they might be willing to work for free, because you want to bless them and respect them for their efforts. They are in need and we need to do more than tell them to be warm, be blessed, and send them on their way. Your response may be, "I shouldn't have to pay them to do something at the church." Consider the heart of Jesus; help meet their need. The prime objective is to spend time with them and get them to talk. If you have to pay for that privilege, count it all joy.

TAKE OUT THE GARBAGE

Don't judge or rail at people to clean up their yard or home. Rather, be willing to help those that ask. Be prepared to pay the dump fees. We found the abundance of this need and the solution required, making it necessary to buy a flat bed trailer for the church.

EMERGENCY SHELTER

Whoo boy, here comes an explosive topic—Emergency Shelter. This is an area many Christians have a tender heart for. Others are violently opposed. So many uninformed, inexperienced opinions come into this discussion. The spectrum of responses range from "sleep in the bed you've made" to functioning as a "homeless shelter."

Homeless people come in all shapes and stories. James teaches us in chapter two of his epistle to put some skin into the game. Some need emergency shelter and others are living the "van life" without a van. A church can provide assistance to the homeless without opening up a shelter. We help the homeless, because we are doing it for Jesus. That simple. Many of the topics of ministry in this chapter can be used to help the homeless. They need food—you have food. They need money—you can have them do some chores and earn the pocket money. They need a job—you can drive them around and help them look. You can print out the classifieds for them. You can help them replace their I.D. You can give them a ride to the DMV or Social Security office. You can let them stay at the church for a couple nights. Before you do, ask them what their plan is. If they have none, help them build one. Otherwise, you'll find yourself in the position of having to kick them out after several days. You can drive them to another city, if that's the solution to the current dilemma. Remember the "car therapy" idea in an earlier chapter—you have a captive audience in your car and time to disciple through conversation. You can connect them to charitable services for food stamps or financial assistance. You can drive them to the medical clinic for care. Your church has internet and you can give them access. They might just need time to communicate with friends, family, or services. Giving them a safe, dry, warm place to hang out to regroup can be life-changing. I would rather pay for the electricity they use or clean the bathroom, than to see them freeze or suffer dehydration. Hang out with them. Some just need the touch of people. Have a spirit of hospitality and generosity.

"Suppose a brother or a sister is without clothes and daily food. If one of you says to them, "Go in peace; keep warm and well fed," but does nothing about their physical needs, what good is it? In the same way, faith by itself, if it is not accompanied by action, is dead." James 2:15-17

CHAPTER 13

Conclusion

Wow! Can you believe what you've just read?

I hope this book has opened your eyes to the intensity of what Jesus called us into. I also hope you have an adventurous spirit that is ready to do ministry outside the box. The Live Among Them method is not a safe way to church. It isn't comfortable. Ministering this way instills a great sense of life purpose. You will be blessed if you make the changes suggested in the book.

After having read this book:

- Do you still think of church in the same way?
- Do you understand the principle of Living Among Them?
- Are you motivated to go to, and live among, the lost, dying, or abandoned?

- Have you gained more confidence to handle requests from the needy?
- Are you scared or intimidated to attempt a Living Among Them ministry and feel you need more hands-on help?

This form of ministry comes with no guarantees. Many of the people to whom you minister won't make the needed changes in their lives. Others will not be healed and some will even die. And thanks be to God, some will be saved. But who and what are we doing this for? We are doing this for Jesus with the hope that those we are helping will get to know Him. We are only responsible for our walk of faith, not the results in other people's lives.

I am available to converse with you by phone, email, or in-person. You are heartily invited to come visit our ministry in Southwest Colorado! I would be willing to visit your church and help you begin, either with a new church or a new approach.

Now that you have all the tools, go out there and use them.

Appendix and Worksheets

- Biblical Basis of Benevolence
- Member Benevolence
- Community Benevolence
- Benevolence Financial Application

You are free to copy and use these.

BIBLICAL BASIS OF BENEVOLENCE

INTERNAL DISCUSSIONS FOR THE MINISTRY

Why Consider Doing This?

As a spiritual body, you may need to raise awareness of the church and engage them in the grace of giving. Decide on a budget for the expenditures and communicate the results as you go. In all likelihood, the church may need to slightly increase regular giving for this new Benevolence fund (if you don't already have one) and possibly Community-Reach.

We need to inspire the non-givers, or occasional givers, to aspire to biblical grace-filled giving. As they respond with giving, what is done with the extra money? This style of exhortation is in contrast to saying, "we have a church need and therefore each of you need to give more money." That is what I'd call deficit motivation rather than biblical motivation. Redirected charitable spending will move the church toward leaders having a larger input on how the treasury is used rather than rely solely on the pastor. These changes reflect new growth of maturity in the church. The church will become a bit more intentional in ministry and in community-mindedness. An intentional community-minded body emulates the biblical practice which contributed to the power and growth of the early church. Along these lines, a change in who does the bookkeeping might be called for due to the increased demands.

What Can We Expect Results to Be?

Church leadership can expect a stronger fellowship and church community. The love and care will be an attractive force for people to stay and new people to come. This will inspire more fervent preaching and teaching among the brethren.

Who Are We To Be Helping?

~ Widows, orphans, the poor within our church and in other churches, along with preacher/teachers may need our help.

We don't have a large contingent of literal widows and orphans in our society. But we do have many single women, single moms who suffer the same problems a widow would. We do have children who are either latch-key kids or cared for by shared parents or grandparents. Kids being cared for by grandparents are likely the closest analogy to orphans we encounter locally.

~ In the early church, the needs of the poor were assisted by the church treasury.

The church received monies from members as they were

able to give and the deacons made distributions. The men of the church who refused to work did not receive support. Widows who did not meet certain expectations did not receive support. Hunger was a large part of the needs of these groups. We do very well at this.

~ The preachers and teachers who dedicated full time effort into the ministry were financially supported.

~ We don't see required giving or great emphasis for buildings in the early church, although we imagine that structures were constructed through community-building. Obviously, the Scriptures don't reveal how much they spent on internet, electricity, and propane, but those needs were met one way or another to minister to the needs of others.

Won't We Be Enabling The Poor? What If We Don't Like The People Receiving Assistance?

Certainly this is the very same issue the first century church had to wrestle with. Some of the men were even using the apostle's teaching of the imminent return of Jesus to quit work and sit around! There were widows who weren't widows indeed. There were widows who had family that could have and should have supported them. There were widows who made no effort to raise a godly family. There were certainly poor people who were intentionally poor. But, God dealt with these issues through the Holy Spirit's words given to the New Testament authors. We will endeavor to use these teachings and err on the side of grace. Those members who just can't stomach the chronic or careless poor can simply choose not to give to this grace account. We will celebrate what God chooses to do and will not chastise those whose faith is "just not there yet" (a fond expression of Bob Hill, late member of Amazing Grace Community Church).

The Model of First-Century Church Spending:

Acts 4:32-35 - Sharing among Believers

"And the congregation of those who believed were of one heart and soul; and not one of them claimed that anything belonging to him was his own, but all things were common property to them. And with great power the apostles were giving testimony to the resurrection of the Lord Jesus, and abundant grace was upon them all. For there was not a needy person among them, for all who were owners of land or houses would sell them and bring the proceeds of the sales and lay them at the apostles' feet, and they would be distributed to each as any had need."

Acts 6:1-3 - Divinely Directed Administration

"Now at this time while the disciples were increasing in number, a complaint arose on the part of the Hellenistic Jews against the native Hebrews, because their widows were being overlooked in the daily serving of food. So the twelve summoned the congregation of the disciples and said, "It is not desirable for us to neglect the word of God in order to serve tables. Therefore, brethren, select from among you seven men of good reputation, full of the Spirit and of wisdom, whom we may put in charge of this task."

2 Corinthians 8:12-15 - Equality that God Desires

"For if the readiness is present, it is acceptable according to what a person has, not according to what he does not have. For this is not for the ease of others and for your affliction, but by way of equality— at this present time your abundance being a supply for their need, so that their abundance also may become a supply for your need, that there may be equality; as it is written, "He who gathered much did not have too much, and he who gathered little had no lack."

James 1:27 - True Religion

"Pure and undefiled religion in the sight of our God and Father is this: to visit orphans and widows in their distress, and to keep oneself unstained by the world."

Scripture Bank

- Treatment of Widows - 1 Timothy 5:3-16
- Supporting full-time Preachers/Teachers - 1 Timothy 5:17,18; Galatians 6:6
- Men who won't work, won't eat - 2 Thessalonians 3:10
- The who, what, when, why, how to give - 2 Corinthians 7-9

    Highlights: Giving is a grace (8:7), Voluntary and a test of sincerity and love (8:8-12; 9:1-2,5,7), Privilege is universal, according to ability, to rich and poor (8:1-3,12-15), Proportioned to income (8:12-14), rewards are increased ability (9:7-11), increased thankfulness (9:12), God and the Gospel glorified (9:13-14).
- First day of the week, weekly - 1 Corinthians 16:1-2

- We must give consistently, generously, and joyfully - 2 Corinthians 9:7
- According to his ability - Acts 11:29
- Stinginess warning - Deuteronomy 15:7-11; 2 Corinthians 9:7; 1 Jn 3:17
- Fellowship (koinonia) as a component of giving - Romans 15:26; 2 Corinthians 8:4; 9:13; Hebrews 13:16

MEMBER'S BENEVOLENCE FUND

This fund is intended for benevolence given to active church members, *not* non-attending community members. Following is an outline of how you might use this at your church. Anyone who is tasked with receiving requests and making decisions should review this.

Process

1. Submit Application to pastor.
2. Submit to deacons for review.
3. Application approved, partially approved, denied or deferred for more information.

Guidelines

1. Applicant must be a regular member of the church (who financially supports the church?) who is visibly making effort to follow the Lord and has been attending at least 6 months before becoming eligible.

2. Applications can only be considered once per year.

3. Monies can only be requested by applicant for applicant (no public or relatives).

4. Deacons and Pastor cannot be decision makers on applications they submit for themselves.

5. The request must be for a need that is reasonable in scale (generally less than $1000), and considered a necessity—not a desire or luxury (e.g. utilities, car payment, funeral, not new TV or cell phone).

6. Medical needs must not be things that insurance or Medicare/Medicaid can pay for or where payments can be arranged. No prescriptions for narcotic or THC based medicines can be paid. Medicare/Medicaid reimbursable travel expenses may be advanced for out of town appointments.

7. No monies can be awarded to help people move out of town.

8. No jail bonds, fines, probation, or testing fees will be paid.

9. Remittances are not loans but gifts from the church.

Church Member Fund Collection Process

1. Separate box or envelopes
2. Promote in church along with guidelines
3. Discerning public reporting made from time to time
4. Monies held in distinct category
5. Fund built up before accepting applications
6. Contributions from church members, not outside supporters

COMMUNITY BENEVOLENCE

Your church could budget or allocate a portion of the treasury to be used for *community benevolence*. Examples are: gas for their car, automotive repair parts, propane to heat their camper, or personal toiletries. These are usually smaller ticket items. I typically have the person in need donate a little of their time doing some chores around the church. Not every situation fits this mold and often we'll just help out with the $25-50 need. I sometimes put the gas in their car or propane tank myself. We rarely buy cigarettes and never marijuana or alcohol (and yes, people ask for these). We often help with prescriptions. When they ask for a loan, say, "No, we are a church, not a bank. If we can't give you the financial help, we aren't going to give you a loan either."

WHAT WE OFFER

1. Food Pantry is offered without qualification,
2. Helping Hands is offered except when the assistance will take away from a business,
3. Rides, employment networking, resource networking is offered without qualification,

4. Financial assistance ($50 and above) is offered pursuant to Biblical guidelines, Crown Financial Ministries Manual, and satisfactory questionnaire. Money is given as charity and not a loan. Checks will be written from the church to the vendor or creditor. Generally, cash is not given out. Ongoing assistance is considered only if recipient is faithfully attending a church, committed to Jesus as Lord and Savior, and taking steps to alleviate the problem area.

COMMUNITY BENEVOLENCE INTERVIEW

Name:

Address:

Telephone:

Email:

Dependents (#/Age):

Marital Status/History:

What is your immediate need? (Please be specific.)

1. Do you attend a church locally? If so, did your church offer you assistance?

2. Where is your church and what is your minister's name?

3. Do you attend AGCC regularly?

4. Do you have relatives who can assist you with your needs?

5. Do you give to AGCC regularly?

6. Are you receiving aid from the government? (unemployment, Social Security, food stamps, worker's comp)?

7. Have you worked a job or looked for work locally? When and where?

8. Are there any obstacles that hinder you from taking a job (child care, disability)?

9. Are you willing to work today if we know of an available job?

10. If we are unable to help you, what other options do you have?

11. If we are able to help you, how many people are involved? (Please list family members.)

12. Do you have some form of identification?

13. Are you willing to engage in financial and spiritual counseling? (If the need is ongoing)

14. Are you willing to do community service or volunteer work?

INTERVIEWER COMMENTS/IDEAS:

FINANCIAL APPLICATION FOR MEMBER ASSISTANCE

Date:

Applicant Name(s):

Address/Phone/Email:

Request:

Cause of Shortfall or Need:

Applicant Financial Snapshot:

Monthly Household Income: $

Sources:

Rent/Mortgage $_____/mo.

Elec $_____/mo.

Propane $_____/mo.

Phone(s) $_____/mo.

Cable $_____/mo.

Internet $_____/mo.

Car Pmt $_____/mo.

Insurance $_____/mo.

Gas $_____/mo.

Credit Card(s) $_____bal

Credit Card Payments $_____/mo.

Health Ins. $_____/mo.

Food (not SNAP) $_____

Alcohol $_____/mo.

Cigarettes $_____/mo.

Marijuana $_____/mo.

Prescriptions $_____/mo

Net Remaining: $_____

Misc. Notes

Section for church decision use

Does Applicant's Request Meet These? (yes / no)

_____ Applicant must be a regular member of the church who is visibly making effort to follow the Lord and have been attending at least 6 months before becoming eligible.

_____ Applicant has been measured by 2 Thessalonians 3:6-15

_____ Applications can only be considered once per year

_____ Monies can only be requested by applicant for applicant (no public or relatives)

_____ The request must be for a need that is reasonable in scale (generally less than $1000),
and considered a necessity—not a desire or luxury (e.g. utilities, car payment, funeral, not new TV or cell phone).

_____ Medical needs must not be things that insurance or medicare/aid can pay for or where
payments can be arranged. No prescriptions for narcotic or THC based medicines can be paid.

_____ Medicare/aid reimbursable travel expenses may be advanced for out of town appointments.

_____ No monies can be awarded to help people move out of town.

_____ No jail bonds, fines, probation, or testing fees will be paid.

Application Notes:

Application taken by: _____

Decision: Approved / Denied / Deferred / More Info

Mark S. Disbrow is the shepherd-pastor of a small mountain church. He is focused on evangelism, discipleship, and life restoration, with a heart for the lost, broken, and abandoned.

Mark and his wife, Adrienne, met each other on the top of Donner Pass (near Lake Tahoe) at a ski bunk-and-breakfast lodge in 1991. Together they live in the Rocky Mountains in Southwest Colorado. They have two adult children and one granddaughter.

Mark's strong interest in, and love of, outdoor recreation, is fulfilled in cross-country skiing, mountain biking (single track), backpacking, camping, mountain climbing, and sledding with kids.

Cover picture was taken by Adrienne Disbrow. If you are interested in her photography and blog, see www.areluctant-pastorswife.com

CPSIA information can be obtained
at www.ICGtesting.com
Printed in the USA
LVHW040602170622
721514LV00011B/936